JOHN **XXIII**

JOHN XXIII

POPE PAUL ON HIS PREDECESSOR
and A DOCUMENTATION BY THE
EDITORS OF 'HERDER CORRESPONDENCE'

HERDER AND HERDER

1965
HERDER AND HERDER NEW YORK
232 Madison Avenue, New York 16, N.Y.

Original editions: *Johannes XXIII. Leben und Werke* (Herder, Freiburg 1963) and *Papa Giovanni XXIII Nella Mente e Nel Cuore del Suo Successore* (Milan 1964). Translated by Salvator Attanasio.

Nihil obstat: Patrick A. Barry
               Censor Librorum

Imprimatur: ✠Robert F. Joyce
             Bishop of Burlington
             June 2, 1964

"Letter to His Brother Zaverio" and "Spiritual Testament" reprinted with permission of McGraw-Hill, Inc. and Geoffrey Chapman, Ltd. from POPE JOHN XXIII: *Journal of a Soul.* © 1965 by Geoffrey Chapman, Ltd.

Library of Congress Catalog Card Number: 64–19731
© 1965 by Herder and Herder, Incorporated
Printed in the United States of America

CONTENTS

JOHN XXIII

ADDRESS BY CARDINAL MONTINI AT THE REQUIEM MASS FOR POPE JOHN IN THE CATHEDRAL OF MILAN, JUNE 7, 1963

Excellencies, gentlemen, dear colleagues and faithful, representatives of the political, civil, military, judicial and academic authorities, citizens, I should like to thank you all most effusively for your spontaneous and reverent presence here in such large numbers. But if the hour does not allow us many words may this gathering of souls, which greatly comforts and honors me and the Church of St. Ambrose, obtain for you abundant spiritual graces and blessings for your participation in an act of mourning which, to your honor, you consider a sorrow to be shared by all. The death of Pope John XXIII has so greatly grieved the Church and has so greatly stirred the world that it has already been described and commented upon and celebrated by thousands of voices. The press, radio, television have made us all participants in this great sorrowful event, offering it to our view, as it were, and to our reflection. Expressions of regret, of praise, of devotion and of remembrance have been proffered from every part of the world. Voices have been raised also in the whole Catholic Church in unanimous and tearful, but at the same time serene and trustful prayer. And

this prayer has been reverently echoed by other Christian
confessions and by members of different religious faiths.
On this night we add the tribute of our sadness, of our admiration, of our prayer to the universal choir, our soul suffused with the majesty and deep emotion with which such a
death has affected everybody. The association of the two attributes, majesty and goodness, i.e. "the good Pope" with
which all mankind has designated and defined the deceased
Pontiff, makes our hearts, seized with rapture by the vision
of greatness and goodness finally conjoined, throb with an
unusual animation. At the same time, however, our hearts
are deeply saddened because the world has been robbed of
this most remarkable and beloved figure. We people of
Milan have special reasons, all of our own, to be stirred and
shaken to the depths of our being. But this too has already
been widely discussed.

Truth and Charity

Everything has already been said on the person of the deceased Pope: on his genuine, simple, innate openness to our
human experience, on his ever cordial affableness, on his
acute and amusing finesse of feeling, on his deep and authentic spirituality. And everything has also been said on
the works of John XXIII, ranging from his opportune and
memorable initiatives which brought him closer to the people, children and especially to the sick and the suffering, to
his great undertakings, the encyclicals and the convocation
of the Second Vatican Ecumenical Council. All this we
know and we will remember.

The religious gathering which unites us here, however, suggests that much still remains to be said and to be meditated upon regarding this Pope who, according to our human feeling, has been untimely removed from the scene of the world. It would be necessary, for example, to investigate and explain the reasons for such a heartfelt and universal sorrow such as that which accompanies John XXIII to his tomb. Why is his death mourned everywhere? And what phenomenon of spiritual unanimity, never seen hitherto, is being produced here below? What, I ask, are the reasons for this?

Each one of us felt the attraction of this man, and has understood that the fondness which was felt for him was not based on an illusion, or on a superficial enthusiasm born of current fashion. Rather, it was a secret which disclosed itself, a mystery which absorbed us. His magic power was another very simple conjunction of two qualities, the union of truth and charity, which shined on our eyes at once marveling and comforted by the sight. He taught us the elementary lesson, yet one so rare and difficult of expression in practice, of the ancient words of St. Paul: "Rather are we to practice the truth in love."

He has made us see that truth, first of all religious truth which is so fragile and delicate even in its inexorable exigencies of language, of conceptualization and of credence, does not exist for itself or in order to divide men and to kindle polemics and dissensions among them. Rather, it exists in order to drawn them into a unity of thought, to serve them with pastoral solicitude, and to suffuse hearts with the joy of the conquest of brotherhood and of divine help. We already knew this, but John XXIII let us enjoy it as a concrete experience. He aroused in us the hope of achieving it and he promised us the fulfillment thereof.

His Legacy

By following the track of these thoughts which intensify our sorrow—his apparition and departure was a fleeting ray of light!—but which also release the flow of an ineffable consolation from the depths of our hearts, by following this track, I say, our eyes open on another horizon illumined by the candid personage of Pope John. We no longer look back, we no longer look upon him, but upon the horizon to which he has opened a path for the Church and for history. If we still wanted to fix our gaze on the tomb, now sealed, we could speak about his legacy which that tomb cannot contain, about the spirit which he infused into our era and which death cannot suffocate. We would then no longer be obliged to describe his past but to foretell the future which he has ushered in. What did John XXIII leave to the Church and to the world that cannot perish with him?

Guidelines

Prophesy is a difficult art. But in this moment this act somehow seems easier and almost obligatory because of the clarity of some premises laid down by the Pope whose death we are mourning. John XXIII marked out some guidelines which it would be wisdom not only to recall but to follow. Could we, perhaps, forget the living demonstration of the

profound, essential capacity of the Christian religion to re-
plenish the modern world with an ever new spiritual energy
which he embodied, in a certain measure, in the extremely
human spontaneity of his saintly life? Allow me to quote at
least one passage from the late Pope John:

"In the oblivion and the weakness surrounding the principles of the natural and supernatural order that character-
ized the penetration and spread of Christian civilization, in
the modern era of a world so deeply altered, straining
mightily to keep its balance amid the temptations and perils
of an almost exclusive search for material goods, it is much
more a question of the substance of human and Christian
thought and life whose custodian the Church has been
down the centuries, and which must again be brought to
recognition and to light, than it is a question of this or that
point of doctrine or discipline which again must be called
back to the pure sources of revelation and tradition. . . ."

Immortal Words

". . . On the other hand it is surely a grave duty to deplore
the wrong ways of the human spirit which is tempted and
driven to the enjoyment merely of the world's goods which
modern scientific research has brought within the reach of
all in our time. May God preserve us, however, from exag-
gerating its dimensions to the point where we are induced
to believe that the heavens of God are now definitively closed
over our heads and that truly darkness has fallen over the
entire earth and that there is naught else for us to do save
to shed tears along our way of vexation. On the contrary,

we must take heart!" (Address to the members and consultors of the Central Preparatory Commission for the council, November 14, 1960).

These are living words, words that death cannot cancel.

Could we deviate from the path he so daringly has opened up to religious history, the path to a greater understanding of the universality of the Catholic faith? From the path of Roman ecumenicism? Pope John personified and expressed this essential attribute of the Catholic Church, universality, in such a way that he thereby awakened hidden energies in the Church herself which unfolded in a double direction, within and without. Not only because he encouraged and fostered the already on-going process of the so-called internationalization of the Church by the spread of missions, or by the increase of relations with old and new nations of the world, or by the admission of persons of every racial provenience to the uppermost hierarchies of the Church and to the central organs of the Holy See. By spontaneously convoking the council, Pope John resumed exploration of the great theme of the fundamental principles of the constitutional structure of the Church, the doctrinal treatment of which had been interrupted by the premature end of the First Vatican Council. Thereby he established the spiritual and practical presuppositions for an harmonious cooperation of the College of Bishops—not in the exercise of the governance of the whole Church, which certainly will remain personal and unitary—but in the responsibility that is connected with it. Thus he laid the basis for the possibility of a canonical development and for a consonant spiritual climate to the inner ecumenicism of Catholic Christianity, making use even here of a binomial, *urbs et orbis*, which had been amicably associated for centuries. Thus conjoined these two realities release astounding energies, pointing the way to new historical development for Rome and perhaps for the papacy itself and for the world.

In his heart and in his work John XXIII combined internal and external ecumenicism which is also dual in character: the effort to bring about the reunion of the so many separated Christian fractions in the organic unity of the faith and charity of the Mother Church, the one, holy, apostolic, catholic Church, and the effort to spread peace between nations, on as broad and enduring a basis as possible, and civil peace among social classes all over the earth.

Could we ever stray from the paths that Pope John has so masterfully traced out, even for the future? I think not! And it will be this loyalty to the great canons of his pontificate which will perpetuate its memory and its glory, and which will make him remain even more paternal and closer to us in the future.

POPE JOHN XXIII (1958–1963)
A DOCUMENTATION OF HIS PONTIFICATE

Upon taking possession of the Lateran Basilica, the Cathedral of Rome, on November 23, 1958 Pope John XXIII declared: "We have no right to see a long way ahead of us." Thereupon he quoted the verse from the hymn of tribulation in the Breviary which is recited at the nones of the ancient Roman day calendar: *"Largire lumen vespere quo vita musquam decidat"* (Grant us light for the evening, and may our life nowhere elude it). After which he added: "There are no surprises, not even the surprises of death for him whose gaze is trustingly turned toward God. Death is holy, because it opens the way to glory and to eternal blessedness." One week later, during a visit to the Roman College of the Propagation of the Faith, he observed: "A month has now passed since the beginning of the pontificate which will take its course to the end of time in a continuation of the pastoral office of St. Peter, after it has but barely touched our person." These remarks indicated that the Holy Father himself did not reckon on a long duration for his pontificate. He was to be proved right in the end.

Nevertheless the documentations that follow will show to

what an extent this brief pontificate has passed over into the history of the Church. Naturally an exposition based chiefly on written documents cannot make the claim that it befittingly points out, let alone appraises the remarkable impact which this Pope especially has had upon the age we live in. Nor can it recreate that aura surrounding Pope John's personality that gave his stewardship of the Petrine office its characteristic stamp and constituted so important an element of the charismatic influence he wielded on so many people after he had been installed, in accord with the so-called prophecies of St. Malachy, as their *"pastor et nauta."*

Curriculum Vitae
of Angelo Giuseppe Roncalli

Angelo Giuseppe Roncalli was born November 25, 1881 in the province and diocese of Bergamo. He was the oldest of ten children of the peasant Giovanni Battista Roncalli and Maria Anna (née Mazzola) Roncalli. Three of his brothers and a sister survived him.

Angelo followed the typical path that is marked out for an Italian boy who is an aspirant to the priesthood. He was eleven years old in 1892, when he entered the Bergamo diocesan seminary. He was allowed to begin his theological studies in Rome, which were interrupted in the following year by a one year obligatory stint in the Italian army. Angelo Roncalli was ordained a priest in Rome August 10, 1904. He celebrated his first Mass before a tiny group of friends and well-wishers. His relatives did not come to Rome for the solemn occasion because the costs of the journey and a stay-over were beyond their means. Upon completing his theological studies, he received the degree of Doctor of Sacred Theology. No sooner however had Angelo embarked on a study of canon law when his bishop, Giacomo Radini-Tedeschi, appointed him his secretary. He served the bishop in this post for ten years, from 1905 to 1914, during which time an intimate relation of mutual affection and trust grew up between them. At the same time Don Angelo Roncalli taught basic theology and Church history at the diocesan seminary. It was during this time that he became interested in the person and achievements of St. Charles Borromeo, an interest which is not without significance in terms of Angelo Roncalli's sacerdotal character. This research resulted in a five-volume work containing documents and correspondence relating to the visitations to Bergamo of the great executor of the Tridentine reforms. The last volume was published after Angelo Roncalli had already been installed in the Chair of Peter as Pope John XXIII.

In June 1915 Don Angelo was called up for military service. In the war he served as a noncommissioned officer with the medical corps of an infantry unit, having been appointed hospital chaplain in 1916. Years later he was to write that his ministrations to wounded soldiers had given him a deep insight into the life and nature of the sacerdotal apostolate. The end of the war found Angelo Roncalli back at his post as professor in the diocesan seminary.

The hour of his call to a ministry of a more encompassing character struck on May 7, 1921 when Benedict XV appointed him director of the Society for the Propagation of the Faith in Italy. His new duties again brought Angelo Roncalli to Rome. After four years in this post he was elevated to archbishop and sent to Bulgaria, where he was entrusted with the difficult and delicate mission of an Apostolic Visitor. Thus began a new period in his career, which later he described as the most fruitful in his life. He opened wide his heart and soul to the lands, the peoples and the Christianity of the East. His marked affection for this part of the world and its populations became a dominant feature of his character. On October 16, 1931 Pope Pius XI elevated him to the rank of Apostolic Delegate to Bulgaria. The very possibility of establishing such a mission, which though not of a diplomatic character actually presupposed and produced political contacts, was in no small measure due to his accommodating and amiable disposition ever open to frank and cordial negotiation. On November 21, 1934 he exchanged this post for that of Apostolic Delegate to Turkey and Greece. This gave him the opportunity to establish new contact with the Greek Orthodox Church and the ecumenical patriarchate of Constantinople, a contact of even greater importance than his previous exposal to the religious world of the East.

Almost exactly ten years later, on December 22, 1944, Pius XII called him to a new field of operation wholly different in configuration and which at that time presented special difficulties. He became the Papal Nuncio to France, whose people at that time were sorely divided and afflicted in the aftermath of German occupation, the Résistance and the end of the war. Beyond and above his specific mission in France Nuncio Roncalli also engaged in efforts to ease

Germany's situation, especially in connection with German
PWS, on which we shall report later. As far as France herself
was concerned his mission here primarily called for an infinite tact and acumen in order to break down the resentment
harbored by broad segments of the population, especially
by leading political groups, against the French episcopate
and the Vatican, who were both severely criticized for
having, at the very least, tolerated the Vichy regime. The
Nuncio successfully met this challenge. He established an
exceedingly friendly relationship with the French people,
among whom his task was to act as the Pope's personal
representative. The fact that during this time he made personal visitations to eighty-five of the eighty-seven French
dioceses is indicative of the far-flung character of this relationship. Crises within the French Church, especially that
revolving around the controversial worker-priest movement,
presented him with many serious problems but they also
confirmed his reputation as a skillful, affable diplomat who
could successfully negotiate thorny issues.

In June 1951 Nuncio Roncalli was further honored by
being appointed the first permanent observer of the Holy
See to UNESCO. Two years later, on January 12, 1953, the
Nuncio was elevated to the dignity of the cardinalate. On
January 12 also, the very same day President Auriol presented him with the cardinal's red biretta, Pius XII named
him Patriarch of Venice, which city he entered in triumph
on March 15. After only a short period in office there he
convoked, as he was later to do in Rome, a diocesan synod.
The restoration of the Cathedral of St. Mark is also a monument to his activity in Venice. Cardinal Roncalli repre-

sented the pope as legate a latere on two further occasions: in October 1954 at the Marian Congress in Beirut and on March 25, 1958 at the centenary celebration of the apparitions at Lourdes, during which time the subterranean Basilica of St. Pius X was consecrated. It was to be his last visit to France.

On October 25, 1958 Cardinal Roncalli entered the conclave, from which he emerged on October 28 as Pope John XXIII. He chose this name in memory of his father and of his parish church. Among other reasons for this choice of name was the fact that all the Pope Johns had reigned for only a short time. He took the words Oboedientia et Pax (Obedience and Peace) as the motto for his coat of arms. His coronation as Pope took place on November 4, the feast of St. Charles Borromeo. Pope John's pontificate lasted four years, seven months and seven days. On Pentecost Monday, June 3, 1963, at 7:49 P.M., Angelo Giuseppe Roncalli went home to his God.

1. "Every pontificate receives its features and its countenance from the person who embodies it and stamps it with his individuality" (from the Coronation homily). These words of the deceased Pope apply to his own pontificate in a special way inasmuch as the influence of this Pope was to a great extent an emanation of his charismatic character. The peasant world from which he came, its simplicity and poverty, its utter dependence on helpful persons and on Him who sends the sun and rain, constituted the foundation of his character. John was aware of the significance of this world in the shaping of his life. In his diaries he wrote: "Having come from the poverty and the simplicity of Sotto il Monte, I have never tried to cut myself off from it." This modesty explains his predilection for simple people, for the humble great figures of the Church, St. Joseph, St. Mark and the Curé of Ars. This early conditioning was further strengthened by the experience of later years, especially during the two world wars. The diaries also make mention of this experience. "I have re-read the book that I wrote at the height of the World War in 1916. The last days of Monsignor Radini, his last invocation: Peace, Peace . . . I would like this to be also my last prayer as Pope."

Pope John's will to serve, to usher in an era of peace and unity, would easily lend itself to a retroactive substantiation on the basis of his childhood experiences and those of his young manhood. Yet such an endeavor would never completely disclose all the many facets of his personality. The charism of this Pope was a felicitous unity of natural and supernatural gifts, conjoined in a rare way, the seamless embodiment of human and historical experience in a deeply pious existence which drew its nourishment wholly out of holy Scripture, to which his addresses and utterances bear continuous witness. Already in his first radio message as Pope on October 30, 1958 he declared: "With fervent fatherly love we embrace the universal Church, the Eastern and Western alike. And we open our heart most lovingly and extend open arms also to all those who are separated from this Apostolic See. . . . Ardently desiring their return to the house of the common Father, we earnestly repeat the words of the Redeemer: 'Holy Father, keep in thy name those whom thou hast given me, that they may be one even as we are' (Jn 17:11)." In the same message, several sentences later, the Pope appealed to the "rulers of all nations." "Why are not divisions and disagreements not settled, once and for all, on a just basis? . . . What is it that people ask of you? Not these new monstrous instruments of war which alarm our time and which can produce fratricidal slaughter and wholesale destruction—not these, but peace, peace . . . Truly it is fitting to ponder and consider with lively attention what the angels sang over the crib of the divine Child: 'Glory to God in the highest, and on earth peace among men of good will' (Lk 2:14). For there is no true peace for the citizen, for nations and races if it first is not granted to their souls . . . In this solemn hour we repeat the words of Christ: 'Peace I leave with you, my peace I give to you' (Jn 14:17)." In the homily delivered at his coronation on November 4, 1958 he posed the question of the ideal Pope as he envisaged the occupant of Peter's Chair. He replied to his own question as follows: "The new Pope, throughout his entire life, is like Joseph the son of Jacob, who had his brothers, all afflicted by grievous misfortune, brought before him and to whom he then lovingly and compassionately disclosed his identity: 'I am Joseph, your brother' (Gn 45:4)." In the same breath he placed alongside the figure of the Old Testament Joseph its fulfillment in the New Testament: the Good Shepherd (Jn 10:1–21). Brother and shepherd in one, this was his ideal of what a Pope should be. In his speeches Pope John repeatedly developed and elaborated this idea with many variations. He returned to the Joseph theme most movingly during an audience which he gave for fifty-five American rabbis, telling them: "I am Joseph, your brother." The Good Shepherd is cited in almost all of his speeches. A deep impulse to brotherhood and to the pastoral ministry incessantly drove him to seek unity and to bring about peace, the very themes he had discussed at length in his first Christmas Message in 1958. All of his Christmas messages dealt with these same themes in their different aspects. In his last Christmas Message, in 1962, Pope John extolled peace and unity in almost hymnal cadences.

He did not evade the responsibility that had been laid upon him to be "*verbum et exemplum*" to his flock (address delivered on the first anniversary of his coronation, 1959). He went among the flock assigned to his care and sought to gain its trust and confidence. Here his simplicity, his natural open-heartedness and a healthy sense of humor proved eminently useful. His forceful, almost blunt speech, totally devoid of any stylization and affectation, especially captivated the hearts of his audiences. There are endless anecdotes about the first days of his pontificate. He visited orphanages and hospitals, spent hours with the prison inmates of Regina Coeli—whom he at once amused and comforted with the story of his uncle who once had to serve a term in jail for poaching. He also asked to be brought before hardened criminals. One of the latter, after the Pope's visit, said that the hour was worth more than a whole encyclical. The unusual form of his pastoral ministry won over the hearts of ordinary folk and gradually even the warm sympathy of those who had adopted a critical "wait and see" attitude. Thus the following excerpt from his diaries may occasion some surprise: "In the first days of this pontifical service I did not fully realize just what it means to be Bishop of Rome and therefore Pastor of the universal Church. Then, week after week, there came full illumination, and I felt at home, as though I had done nothing else during my whole life." We can understand this self-criticism only in the sense that he was not clear as to how he could become a shepherd of souls, despite all the contacts which he had with the population and which he maintained throughout the following years, by leaving his retinue during his trips through Rome and mixing with the people in the nearby streets ("Don't applaud so much," he warned frequently, "so that we can talk longer.").

He was the first to reintroduce public worship at the stational churches in Rome for the Sundays of Lent, which had not been celebrated there since the fifteenth century. John led the procession on foot, singing and praying as bishop among his flock, before the various stational churches of the city. This procession deeply stirred the people of Rome. The impact of the Lenten procession was intensified even further when Pope John, for the first time since Pius IX, publicly performed the ceremony of the washing of the feet on Maundy Thursday. On Good Friday he took part in the veneration of the cross in Santa Croce di Gerusalemme (it was on this occasion that "pro perfidis Judaeis" was replaced simply by "pro Judaeis") and on Easter night he personally recited the prophecies and consecrated the baptismal water. Similarly and with equal success Pope John also reintroduced the public Corpus Christi procession in his bishopric. He not only issued decrees to his flock, he mingled among them. A Corpus Christi procession had not been seen on the streets of Rome since 1724. One year later the Bishop stepped beyond the borders of the inner city. During the Lenten season he celebrated the holy mysteries with the workers of the Centocelle, Tiburtina and the Garbatella quarters. The necessity of adapting the pastoral ministry to the changed conditions of modern Rome induced him to convoke and preside over the diocesan synod, the first in the city's history. This synod will be discussed elsewhere at greater length. All this was new for Rome and quite unexpected. Nevertheless the situation favored such trends and time had paved the way. The grievous tensions between the Italian government and the Vatican were things of the past; the legacy of fascism, of the war and of the first post-war crises that had cast their shadows over the pontificates of Pius XI and Pius XII had largely been erased. The Bishop of Rome vigorously seized the opportune moment and he was not disappointed. The Pope's journey on October 4, 1962 through the territory of a former Papal State to Assisi and Loreto was the most visible expression of the new relationship between Church and state.

Shepherd of the World

2. What Rome and the world experienced in the first years of the pontificate of John XXIII in many ways corresponded to the goals which the Pontiff had set himself in terms of his view of himself as brother and shepherd to all: sanctification through helpful example and modesty. Thus he requested the editor of *L'Osservatore Romano* to discontinue publishing pictures of him in the future. And he personally deleted all adjectives that referred flatteringly to his person and pontificate in one of his biographies that was being prepared for publication in Germany. But frequently his actions were not yet understood in this self-effacing sense by the world. There was rejoicing over the "new style," the "fresh air" in the Vatican, the dispensing with protocol, with hoary tradition, with red tape. On the other hand people all too easily turned up their noses—especially in the countries beyond the Alps—over many of the Pope's administrative measures. In other words, most people were delighted with the new shepherd. Gladly they held him in high esteem in that role, but in some matters they felt differently about the helmsman steering Peter's Bark.

In part this was due to the long habituation to a rigid administration by the central authorities of the Church. Thus no matter how much one might have sighed under the old governance there was a reluctance to dispense with its visible results. Moreover the Pope's personality was another factor contributing to this sense of dismay over the direction of the Church. One of his friends had once described him as a man who delighted in making sudden decisions, but who at the same time could turn things over in his mind at great length before taking any action.

In short, the Pope was a man who on the one hand could be decisively and vigorously direct concerning matters of crucial importance and patient and detached concerning matters of a secondary order. Many proofs of this attitude toward decision-making can be adduced from the Pope's life, as well as from his relations with the curial congregations. He did not attach an importance to things which would be disproportionate to their importance in reality. Least of all did he attach a great importance to his own person. Once he told a bishop that when he could not sleep at night because of his concern over Church matters, he would let "the Pope" say: "Angelo, don't take yourself too seriously." Thus there was the impression that at times the guidance of the Church might slip out of the Pope's hands. Needless to say, however, the whole history of Pope John's pontificate has proved the erroneousness of such an assumption. At a comparatively early date Pope John had already discussed the question of employing exceptional means for exceptional situations in his address to the Latin American bishops on November 15, 1958. This address is extraordinarily instructive as regards his manner of Church governance. Reduced to a formula, the means recommended by the Pope are: look, judge, act.

They are therefore the same means he was to propose two years later in his encyclical *Mater et Magistra*. The second proposition underlying the address is even more indicative of his view of Church government. "We must clearly and firmly undertake," said the Pope, "a twofold program: we could call the first 'a long range' program, whereas the second must be actualized immediately."

There are sufficient indications that these two proposals as regards method were the fruit of the Pope's long historical studies. Usually he prefaced his speeches and addresses with historical and personal reminiscences. Two of his encyclicals briefly touch upon biographies of great saints. With an almost conversational informality he showed how history unfolds in the concrete situation and how individuals can meaningfully influence the shaping of history in the interests of the welfare of the Church and of mankind. This explains the wholly unique tone of his doctrinal writings, which bear the dual imprint of history and personal experience. The Pope knew that not everything which should be striven for can be achieved at any time and in any situation. One must be satisfied with more modest goals. The possible is always the best (see *Princeps pastorum*). Nevertheless what may be possible at any specific time must be ascertained through trial and error. As Bishop of Rome and shepherd of the world John XXIII ventured to embark precisely on such a program of trial and error and paved the way to success. Neither the preparations for the council, nor the beginnings of its proceedings, nor his last attempts to come to the assistance of the 65,000,000 Catholics behind the Iron Curtain are understandable unless one takes into account his lofty and venturesome spirit. This spirit was born of his deep trust in God and of his faith in the essential goodness of man—both of which had been confirmed by his own experience. His optimism grew apace when he was able to confirm that his efforts promised to bear fruit. Thus on the occasion of the opening of the second meeting of the Central Preparatory Commission of the council, on November 7, 1961, he said: "On the basis of the fact that the influence which the Church and her documents exert on the whole world strongly affects not only Catholics but also those outside the Church, who for that very reason could be less concerned with her utterances, we may draw the conclusion that this zeal does not flag but increases the more anxiety and skepticism grow. . . ." In the Apostolic Constitution *Humanae salutis,* promulgated on December 25, 1961, he wrote: "Yes, we would like to make ours Christ's injunction to read 'the signs of the times' (Mt 16:4) and therefore believe to see in all the encircling darkness not a few signs which encourage the hope of a better future for the Church and human society." He attributed the causes that had engendered this hopefulness to the two wars, to the harm wrought by false ideologies and to the awesome instruments of war that had been forged by scientific progress. "The present state of affairs,

so ridden with care and anxiety, has led man to sober reflection . . . All this doubtlessly facilitates the apostolic work of
the Church. For many, who hitherto perhaps had no knowledge of her lofty mission, are, after the bitter lesson of
experience, today more likely to hearken to her admonition." The Pope's optimism was most clearly expressed in
his opening address to the council on October 11, 1962:
"In the daily exercise of our pastoral office, we sometimes
have to listen, much to our regret, to voices of persons who,
though burning with religious zeal, are not endowed with
too much a sense of discretion or measure. In these modern
times they can see nothing but prevarications and ruin.
They say that our era, in comparison with past eras, is
getting worse, and they behave as though they had learned
nothing from history, which is sometimes the teacher of
life, and as though at the time of former councils everything was a full triumph for the Christian idea and life, and
for proper religious liberty. We feel we must disagree with
those prophets of gloom. In the present order of things
Divine Providence is leading us to a new order of human
relations which, by men's own efforts and even beyond
their very expectations, are directed toward the fulfillment
of God's superior and inscrutable designs, and everything,
even human differences, leads to the greater good of the
Church."

These excerpts give us a clear understanding of the sense
in which Pope John viewed history as a teacher of mankind.
His primary concern in the study of history was to perceive
how Providence was made manifest and ultimately prevailed in time. He entertained no illusions that everybody

would immediately take an understanding view of his bold
venture to smooth the way for the will of God. After the
promulgation of *Pacem in terris* he made the following
entry in his diary: "The world has awakened. Slowly, slowly
the pure doctrine of the encyclical will find its way into
consciences. No, I am not grieved by what is written and
said about me. It is all too little when compared with the
sufferings of Jesus, Son of God, during all His life and on
the Cross." The Pope shouldered the responsibility for any
misunderstanding of his intentions. He knew that the fath-
oming, the rendering visible, the execution of God's plans,
and the changing of the *status quo ante* would at first always
engender divisions and dissensions. He was ready to sacrifice
his life for it. During his last illness he confided to his diary:
"This bed is an altar, the altar demands a victim. Here I am,
ready. I have before me the clear vision of my soul, of my
priesthood, of the council, of the universal Church."

The Council

3. How did Pope John view the council, the universal
Church? If we consult the many pronouncements and utterances that he made in the course of almost four years, it
can be established that his view on this matter was not
formed whole in all its details from the very outset. Rather
it evolved gradually, undergoing revisions shaped by conditions and situations to which the Pope, in details, accommo-
dated himself, but never losing sight of the great aim he
had set himself. No complete documentation of the council,
since it is available elsewhere, will be provided here. We

will limit ourselves exclusively to an attempt to acquire insights into the thought and the deeds of the deceased Pope, as well as into his conception of the mission of the Church in our time, on the basis of the events that took place at the council and of the work of preparation leading up to its historic convocation.

The Pope had taken it upon himself to accomplish three great tasks during his pontificate: the convocation of the ecumenical council and of the Roman diocesan synod, and the new codification of Canon Law, which he announced on January 25, 1959. The Pope personally directed the preparatory work and the completion of the first session, and the activities marking the interim period prior to the second session. As regards the third task he did not go beyond the setting-up of a commission. But he was able to preside from beginning to end over the Roman diocesan synod. On January 25, 1959 the Pope clearly explained that both projects grew "out of the twofold task that is entrusted to a successor of St. Peter" . . . "from my twofold responsibility as the Bishop of Rome and as the shepherd of the universal Church." Later he repeatedly stated that he regarded the Roman diocesan synod as a model for the subsequently convoked council. He stressed this point more explicitly on June 28, 1960, in his address on the occasion of the promulgation of the synodal statutes: "The synod aspires to be a first step in the direction of a celebration which will be of enormous importance for the whole Church, namely toward the Second Vatican Council." Despite the vast difference between the two events, some disclosures regarding his views of the council's work of

internal Church reform, and even more of the new codification of canon law planned by the Pope, can be garnered
from a study of the proceedings and the results of the synod,
which in Pope John's view had achieved its basic aims.
Since synodal statutes are codifications of law these views
can be obtained solely by an exact textual comparison with
a corresponding codification of Church law, the CIC, which
is still in force. Such a comparison has been made by Ivo
Fürer, a summary of which was published in the periodical
Civitas (January 1962).

In contrast to the CIC the synodal statutes view the ideal
priest in terms of a fundamental orientation to pastoral care.
Even the religious order is viewed as apostolically oriented,
whereupon the direct and indirect inclusion of the order in
pastoral work logically follows. The synodal definitions contain no texts on trial procedures and penalties. The privileges of the clergy are not dealt with—indeed the word
"privilege" is not even mentioned. In contrast to the CIC
the dignity and the tasks of the laity in the Church and in
the world are outlined and elucidated. Great importance is
attached to an effective coordination of available energies
and to proper planning. The synodal statutes are not de-
fensive; rather they take a positive attitude toward modern
possibilities and opportunities, the perils of which are
pointed out only as a secondary matter. Mildness prevails
in the attitude toward persons who are excommunicated
and suspended from the Church. Repeatedly the statutes
stress that Church progress is to be expected less from
sensational innovations than from spiritual deepening and
from a sense of responsibility for bringing about the king-

dom of God. The unified coordination of all energies is viewed as more important than any urgent desire for reform in individual areas.

Surely it may be validly assumed that the spirit which emanates from the statutes of the Roman synod should also ultimately shape the work of the council, in accordance with the wishes and the will of the Pope.

In his diary the Pope described the origins of his three-fold plan: the council, the synod and the new codification of the CIC. "I mentioned the words ecumenical council, the diocesan synod and the reform of canon law in an earlier talk with my secretary of state on January 20, 1959 without ever having given it any thought before and in a way that contrasted to everything that I had previously proposed or imagined at this point. . . . I myself was the first to be surprised by my proposal before anyone else was in a position to give signs of his reaction." In his address to Venetian pilgrims on May 8, 1962 the Pope described the origin of the plans to hold a council with similar words. They were supplemented by the important disclosure that on that day he had asked the then state secretary, Cardinal Tardini, whether in view of the world situation "the Church should be at the mercy of the tides" or whether the people should not expect from her "the light of a great example," and not only admonitions.

"The Church at the mercy of the tides." This was Pope John's appraisal of the actual situation of the Church in the modern world. His words may certainly be interpreted to the effect that in his view the Church was no longer where she ought to be in accordance with her mission. This awareness led Pope John to announce the convocation of the council on January 25, 1959. The verbatim text of the address, which was impromptu and delivered extemporaneously, will never be fully ascertained because the address delivered in San Paolo fuori le Mura was not immediately published. The communique published in the *L'Osservatore Romano* (January 26–27, 1959) reads: "As regards the celebration of the ecumenical council it should, according to the Pope's view, serve for the edification of Christian people; at the same time the council should also be an invitation to the separated communities to seek unity . . ."

The twofold task assigned to the council was confirmed by the Pope himself on January 30, 1959. Indeed the Pope even gave special emphasis to the thrust toward "unity" when he told the parish priests of Sts. John and Paul Church: "We do not wish to hold an historical trial; our aim is not to point out who was right and who was wrong. The responsibility is shared on both sides. We want merely to say: let us come together, let us put an end to the divisions."

The first precise suggestion as to just how the way could be paved for promoting the unity of separated Christians followed in his speech to the Venetian clergy on April 24, 1959: "As regards the East, there must first be a rapprochement, then a coming together and finally perfect unity of so many separated brethren with the ancient, common Mother. As for the West, there must be magnanimous pastoral cooperation between both clergies, the secular priesthood and the religious in the orders, both under the watchful eye and guidance of the bishop. . . ." It is striking that this address did not yet contain any mention of separated Christians of the West.

After the establishment of the first pre-preparatory commission (*commissione antipreparatoria*) on the feast of Pentecost 1959, which ushered in the first phase of the preparations for the council, there came a further clarification of the council's goals in Pope John's address to the Pontifical Greek College on June 14, 1959. According to this address the Holy Father had from the outset intended that the council should exclusively concern itself with the Catholic Church. The Church must adapt herself to new circumstances. The word "aggiornamento" was first used in this context. Many changes have been wrought in the modern world, both among the faithful and in the way of life which they must lead. When the Church accomplishes this aggiornamento she will then be able to turn to the separated brethren and say: See, this is what the Church is, this is what she is doing, this is how she looks. Only when the Church is thus modernized to a healthy degree and rejuvenated can she turn to the separated brethren and say: Come to us. "Today it is clear that it is impossible and futile to begin discussions that would lead nowhere."

Accordingly in his first encyclical *Ad Petri cathedram* the Pope outlined the council's aim as follows: "The principal aim of the council is to promote the development of the Catholic faith, to renew the Christian life of the faithful and to adapt ecclesiastical discipline to the needs and conditions of our time. The council will surely be a wonderful manifestation of truth, unity and charity. It will indeed be a manifestation which we hope will be received by those who are separated from this Apostolic See as a gentle invitation to seek and find that unity for which Jesus Christ prayed so ardently to His heavenly Father."

John XXIII underlined the sequence of the council's goals in his allocution to the diocesan directors of Italian Catholic Action on August 1, 1959.

In his 1960 Pentecost message, immediately after the promulgation of the Motu proprio *Superno Dei nutu*, which ushered in the second and concluding phase of the preparations for the council—the formation of the commissions and of the Secretariat for Promoting Christian Unity, as well as of the Central Preparatory Commission—the Pope made two further stipulations with respect to the Council:

1. The ecumenical council has its own structure and organization which must not be confused with the regular and characteristic functions of the different authorities and congregations which make up the Roman Curia . . . A clear distinction exists here: the regular government of the Church is one thing, the council another.
2. The ecumenical council is constituted by the presence and participation of bishops and prelates who are the living representation of the universal Catholic Church . . .

Summarizing and further developing these viewpoints and stipulations at the beginning of the second phase of the preparation for the council, on November 14, 1960, the Pope declared:

The ecumenical councils of the past primarily provided answers to the most diverse of pressing questions of pure doctrine concerning the "*lex credendi*," with respect to heresies and errors . . . In the modern era, in a world so deeply altered, . . . it is much more a question of the substance of human and Christian thought and life whose custodian and teacher the Church has been down the centuries, a fact which must again be brought to light and recognized by all, than it is a question of this or that point of doctrine or discipline which must again be traced back to the pure sources of revelation and tradition. . . . The council however has a limitation peculiar to it alone. As a "city on the mountain" it must first of all deal exclusively with what concerns our Mother, the Catholic Church, and her present-day internal organization . . . The celebration of a council of the Catholic Church includes the study of a whole complex of relations not only on the plane of individuals and families, but also on that of nations on whom the coexistence of man rests.

In the same speech the Pope, referring to the tasks of the Secretariat for Promoting Christian Unity, said that he had provided for a secretariat "that could answer with the requisite prudence and gracious tact the requests coming from the side of our brethren who though separated—as we are wont to say—are nevertheless most worthy of our attention if they have the desire to follow the work of the council in the light of truth."

In his closing address to the first session of the Central Preparatory Commission of the council, on June 12, 1961, Pope John succinctly formulated the aims of the council as follows: "That the clergy of all ranks shine forth in a new holiness, that the Christian truths and commandments be proclaimed to the people of God in the most appropriate way possible, that the new younger generation hold fast to a righteous life, that the work of the social apostolate be promoted and that missionary zeal be strengthened, that is to say, the zealousness of all to show themselves as brothers and friends." Thereupon the Pope asked: "What is the situ-

ation with regard to our beloved brethren who are separated
from the fold of the Church? What is the situation with regard to the great number of people who do not bear the sign
of Christ on their foreheads and who are nevertheless God's
offspring?" Again, he answered his own question: "You
should be certain that we rightly appraise their voices and
their attentiveness. Even in this respect the council is not a
gathering for the discussion of speculative matters, but a
living organism, which directs its gaze upon the whole
world and embraces it. It is the House . . . it is the Church,
which invites all people to her bosom."

The Pope returned to the subject of the council and separated Christians once more in the encyclical *Aeterna Dei*:
"We firmly trust that such a solemn gathering of bishops
will not only strengthen and solidify that unity in faith, in
worship and in leadership . . . but that it will also attract the
attention of all those who bear the name of Christian and
summon them all to gather around 'the great Pastor of the
sheep' (Heb 13:20) who entrusted the guidance of his
flock to Peter and his successors forever (see Jn 21:15–17)."

All points of view concerning the character of the council
and the reasons for its convocation were once more summarized in the Apostolic Constitution *Humanae salutis*,
promulgated December 25, 1961. Special emphasis was
given the necessity for an elucidation of the fundamental
truths for smoothing the way for the separated brethren.
The council was assigned a further concrete task, namely
"to offer all men of good will in the whole world, burdened
with uncertainty and anxiety engendered by the constant
eruption of new and frightful conflicts, an opportunity to

work out proposals for achieving peace and to smooth the way for their actualization."

The Pope's radio message to the Catholic world on September 11, 1962 was almost exclusively dedicated to this last and third set of subjects on the council's agenda. He dwelt only briefly on the internal expressions of Church life (*ad intra*). On the other hand he discussed their external expressions (*ad extra*) at great length and on a moving note of imploration: the necessity for finding a solution to pressing social problems, church-state relations, the right to freedom, justice and peace. The gathering of the Fathers answered the Pope's call in their first conciliar message to the world on October 20, 1962. In this message they expressed their readiness to promote peace and justice through a ministry of love.

In his memorable address at the opening of the council, on October 11, 1962, the Pope finally gave the assembled Fathers an insight into what he understood by a defense and propagation of doctrine:

The twenty-first ecumenical council, which will draw upon the efficacious and important wealth of juridical, liturgical, apostolic and administrative experience, wishes to transmit the doctrine, pure and integral, without any attenuation or distortion which throughout twenty centuries, notwithstanding difficulties and contrasts, has become the common patrimony of men. It is a patrimony not well received by all but always a rich treasure available to men of good will.

Our duty is not only to guard this precious treasure, as if we were concerned only with antiquity, but to dedicate ourselves with an earnest will and without fear to that work which our era demands of us, pursuing thus the path the Church has followed for twenty centuries . . .

The salient point of the council is not, therefore, a discussion of one article or another of the fundamental doctrine of the Church, which has repeatedly been taught by the fathers and the ancient and modern theologians and which is presumed to be well-known and familiar to all. For this a council was not necessary. But from the renewed, serene and tranquil adhesion to all the teaching of the Church in its entirety and preciseness as it still stands resplendent in the acts of the Councils of Trent and Vatican I, the Christian, Catholic and apostolic spirit of the whole world expects a step forward toward a doctrinal penetration and a formation of consciences, in faithful and perfect conformity with the authentic doctrine which, however, should be studied and expounded through the methods of research and through the literary forms of modern thought. . . . One thing is the substance of the ancient doctrine of the *Depositum Fidei* and another is the way in which it is presented. And it is this that must be taken into great consideration with patience, if necessary, everything being measured in the forms and proportions of a magisterium that is prevalently pastoral in character.

In reference to the errors of our time and the problem of overcoming them, the Pope declared:

Ever has the Church opposed . . . errors. Frequently she has condemned them with the greatest severity. Nowadays, however, the spouse of Christ prefers to make use of the medicine of mercy rather than that of severity. She considers that she meets the needs of the present day by demonstrating the validity of her teaching rather than by condemnations.

Not, certainly, that there is a lack of fallacious teaching of opinions and dangerous concepts to be guarded against and dissipated, but they are so evidently in contrast with the right norm of honesty, and have produced such lethal fruits, that by now it would seem that men of themselves are inclined to condemn them. . . .

Even more important, experience has taught men that violence inflicted on others, the might of arms and political domination are of no help at all in finding a happy solution to the grave problems that afflict them.

Once again the Pope deplored that the "entire Christian family has not yet fully attained visible unity in truth." He also voiced sorrow that "the greater part of the human race —although all men who are born were redeemed by the blood of Christ—does not yet participate in those sources of divine grace that exist in the Catholic Church."

In summing up the Pope said: "Such is the aim of the ecumenical council Vatican II which, while bringing together the Church's best energies and striving to have men welcome more favorably the good tidings of salvation, prepares, as it were, and consolidates the path toward that unity of mankind which is required as a necessary foundation in order that the earthly city may be brought to resemble that heavenly city . . ."

On the basis of these views of the Pontiff, which he gradually elaborated and refined, regarding the tasks of the council in relation to the problems of our time, it becomes clear that he did not want to see the efforts of the Church restricted solely and exclusively thereto. Rather, in accordance with her nature, the Church should seek the way to the hearts of the separated brethren and to anxiety-ridden mankind groaning under its burdens, the way that had already been traversed by her Founder and Teacher. Salvation lies in the reexperience and in the deepening of his testament.

A close reading of all the documents promulgated during the last two years of Pope John's pontificate justifies the assertion that the third theme or topic for discussion—the relation between the council and the world—to which he directed the council to give its special attention, assumed a greater importance in his mind in the course of time. In his

own lifetime Pope John was granted the satisfaction of veri-
fying, as proved by the enthusiastic worldwide response to
Mater et Magistra and *Pacem in terris*, that the Church is
neither an appendage of temporal movements nor their un-
popular opponent, but a pioneer of fundamental change.

The mode and manner with which the Pope steered toward his great goal can be gathered directly only from his
addresses. Hence in this connection it is instructive to see
what the Pope did during the three years that went into the
preparation of the council, and during and after the first
session, and how he conducted himself during these phases.
The path leading from the proclamation of the council on
January 20, 1959, which came like a bolt out of the blue, to
its formal opening on October 11, 1962 was broad and difficult and not entirely free of opposition and obstacles.

The Pope proceeded prudently, lending a hand circum-
spectly and decisively when necessary. He wanted a council
of the whole Church. Therefore he called upon the episco-
pates, the religious orders, universities and theological facul-
ties of the whole world to make known their wishes and to
express their opinions. The Pope was experienced enough in
these matters to know that the material collected, and to be
collected, whose bulk encompassed ten thick folio volumes,
could not be possibly worked through in the time period
that he had fixed. Thus the Pope gave a free hand to the ten
commissions preparing the schemas. He did not even interfere when disagreements developed between individual preparatory commissions. His guidance of the Central Preparatory Commission in connection with the processing of the
schemata was anything but strict. He did not prevent vari-

ous curial congregations from indulging in attempts to prejudice and impede the work of the council through decrees and ordinances of their own. The Pope proved to be unyielding only on one point: the council must take place despite the curia (*"Il concilio si deve fare malgrado la curia"*). Consequently he pushed through the timetable that he had provided for.

At first he did not interfere in the work of the first session. The debates tended to longwindedness. But the Pope allowed them to continue in their interminable way. Why? He was aware of the fact that for the first time in the history of the Church the council was a forum of the Fathers of the whole world, of a Church that today truly stretched to the furthermost ends of the earth. The expansion of the Church during the last fifty years had taken place with extreme swiftness under the pressure of international political developments. Cross-connections, when they were at all possible, could be effected only with great difficulty and in a purely external way. An important if not the most momentous consequence of that development was the divergence between the different trends and schools within the doctrinal framework of the universal Church, without this split being fully realized on the Church periphery. Even more serious was the fact that the different views of a theological and pastoral character rigidly opposed one another, without there being a conciliation of these conflicting views, a division which consequently engendered a weakening of the impetus and will to apostolic activity. The Pope had always seen himself as being everyone's Pope. Thus for precisely this reason he wanted this assembly of Fathers to become

aware of the situation of today's Church in the very encounter and disputations between the various viewpoints.
He was convinced that a purified image of the Church in
the total configuration of the contemporary world could be
obtained only from a knowledge of the reasons for the dis-
placement of the Church in the modern world, indeed for
the ineffectiveness of her proclamations. The Pope's de-
scription of the Church as "being at the mercy of the tides"
could have had no other meaning.

The Pope's decisive intervention occurred November 20,
1962 when he put aside the schema on the sources of revelation despite the fact that a two-thirds majority was lacking.
He then appointed a new commission to work out a new
schema, under the direction of Cardinals Ottaviani and Bea.
On December 4 the gathering of Fathers, through their
spokesman Cardinal Suenens, professed their adherence to
the twofold task of the council along the lines which had
been laid down by the Pontiff himself several times during
the previous months: namely the Church *ad intra* and the
Church *ad extra* in a drastically changed world. Immediately
after the first session therefore conciliar materials were con-
solidated, and mixed commissions as well as a coordinating
commission were set up. In short, the necessary transmis-
sional apparatus was established for the fruitful preliminary
and subsequent work in connection with the second session.
This intermediate conciliar apparatus zealously set to work.
Subsequently the Pope died and the council was suspended.

Up to now the council has remained a work that is only
partially completed. Despite this fact it has produced results
that no one would have ventured to imagine before the

opening of the council. Manifestly Divine Providence had allotted this man, under whose name the twenty-first council would go down in history, just enough time to make the intentions of his pontificate visible to the whole world: the opening of the Church outwards, on all sides and fronts, *per verbum et exemplum:* I am the Good Shepherd, I am Joseph, your brother. By the same token Divine Providence had allotted him so brief a time span in order to show that with God nothing is impossible.

After Pope John's death the Fathers of the Church proclaimed their ardent support of the Pontiff's program. They extolled his pontificate as the beginning of a new epoch in the history of the Church. One of the cardinals, who arrived in Rome immediately after the Pope's death, declared: "As far as the future is concerned, it is a question of continuing what has already been undertaken in such a way that it really becomes something new without thereby weakening the connection with the past."

Pope John as a person had no adversaries. But much of what he did and proposed encountered much opposition.

A newspaper of esteemed international reputation summarized this inevitable fate of every great historical contribution to its age as follows: "The force emanating from the person of Pope John had a powerful impact on minds. His pontificate can be judged only after many years have passed. We know that historical success does not lend itself to measurement on the basis of the number of shouts of Hosannah. Supreme shepherds, to whom posterity has erected monuments of gratitude, in their lifetime suffered insults from the world similar to those endured by their divine Master."

Following the Pope's death periods of official national mourning were declared in many countries, among others The Philippines, Lebanon, Spain, Portugal, Italy, Liechtenstein and several Latin American countries, including Cuba and Brazil. The sympathy shown by the Roman, French, North American and Polish peoples and many others during the last days of the agonized Pope, and upon his death, was overwhelming. Flags flew at halfmast even in Buckingham Palace, the residence of the head of the Church of England and Scotland, as well as in the glass palace of the United Nations. The World Council of Churches, the representatives of world Jewry and of the Moslem nations eulogized the deceased Pontiff in moving and grateful tributes.

Sources

On the person of the Pope and the character of his pontificate: coronation homily, AAS 1958, 884–888; Occupancy of the Lateran Basilica, AAS 1958, 909–921; First radio message, AAS 1958, 838–841; Christmas Message 1958, AAS 1959, AAS 1959, 5–12; Christmas Message 1959, AAS 1960, 27–35; Christmas Message 1960, AAS 1961, 5–15; Christmas Message 1961, AAS 1962, 46–48; Christmas Message 1962, AAS 1963, 13–19; Easter Message, 1961, AAS 1961, 193–197; Easter Message 1962, AAS 1962, 291–295; Pentecost homily 1962, AAS 1962, 437–447; address on the first anniversary of his coronation, 1959, AAS 1959, 814–818; address to the Latin American Bishops' Conference, AAS 1958, 997–1005; encyclical Sacerdotii nostri primordia, AAS 1959, 545–579; encyclical Aeterna Dei, AAS 1961, 758–803; encyclical Princeps pastorum, AAS 1959, 497–531; encyclical Pacem in terris, AAS 1963, 257–304; address to the second session of the Central Preparatory Commission of the council, *AAS* 1961, 728–731; Apostolic Constitution *Humani salutis*, *AAS* 1962, 5–13; opening address to the council, *AAS* 1962, 786–796.

On the revision of canon law: The Commission for the Revision of the Codex of Canon Law, *AAS* 1963, 363–364.

On the Roman diocesan synod: announcement of the synod, *AAS* 1959, 65–69; address to the synod, *AAS* 1960, 180–309; promulgation of the statutes, *AAS* 1960, 551–554, 563–567.

On the Second Vatican Council (the most important documents): announcement of the council, *AAS* 1959, 65–69; address to the representatives of Catholic universities, *AAS* 1959, 299–301; address to the Venetian clergy, *AAS* 1959, 375–381; appointment of the pre-preparatory Commission, *AAS* 1959, 419–422; address delivered on Pentecost 1959, *AAS* 1959, 419–422; Motu proprio *Superno Dei nutu*, *AAS* 1960, 433–437; address to the consistory, January 16, 1961, *AAS* 1961, 66–70; Brief on the feast of St. Joseph 1961, *AAS* 1961, 205–213.

Address to the first session of the Central Preparatory Commission of the council, *AAS* 1961, 729–733; encyclical *Aeterna Dei*, *AAS* 1961, 785–803; Apostolic Constitution *Humani salutis*, *AAS* 1962, 5–13; Motu proprio *Consilium*, *AAS* 1962, 65–66; concluding address to the third session of the Central Preparatory Commission of the council, *AAS* 1962, 97–101; Exhortatio Apostolica *Sacrae Laudis*, *AAS* 1962, 66–75.

Encyclical *Paenitentiam agere*, *AAS* 1962, 481–491; Motu proprio *Appropinquante concilio*, *AAS* 1962, 609–631; radio message to the Catholics of the world, *AAS* 1962, 678–685.

Message on the opening of the council, *AAS* 1962, 786–795; address to the observers at the council, *AAS* 1962, 814–819; address to the government delegations, *AAS* 1962, 807–810; epistole *Mirabilis ille*, *AAS* 1963, 149–159.

The Office of Dogmatic Teaching

The pontificate of John XXIII produced definite pronouncements relating to theological questions. But a clear distinction must be made here between documents of a canonical tradition and his utterances of a nondefined theology. The former to a large extent were worked out by the competent curial authorities, whereas the latter were expressed in an apostolic and missionary spirit during the preparations for the ecumenical council and, later, during its proceedings. The Pope's pastoral ministry stood at the center of his whole activity. His aim was not only to recast the truths that have been handed down through the centuries, or merely to repeat them. The Pope also tried to find new forms both for the preaching of the gospel and for the actual signs of God, to which the pastoral office of the Church and the Pope must first of all pay heed.

1. The missionary mandate to achieve the unity of the Catholic Church as willed by Jesus Christ was the pedal note of his theology, both in a traditional and a modern sense. This unity is unity in Christ, unity according to the Church's hierarchical structure, the unity of Catholics, the unity of all Christians, indeed of all peoples and races, the unity of peace and brotherhood. Such was the general

theme of Pope John's addresses to the world on Christmas, Easter and Pentecost. Peace was constantly viewed both as a theologico-prophetic and political goal. Pseudo-peace was rejected. Voiced here was a strong hierarchic consciousness of the role of Peter's successor, of the bishop, without whom no one can wholly be united with Christ (to Cardinal Tien, June 29, 1961). This concept of hierarchical order was most emphatically formulated in *Ad Petri cathedram*, as though the words "I am Joseph, your brother" had never been uttered.

Nevertheless the Pope avoided talking about the rights and prerogatives of the Church whenever possible. But he was eloquent in portraying the ministration of the Church to mankind, her ability to be of assistance at all times of crisis and tribulation out of the fullness of her love (for example *Mirabilis ille*, January 6, 1963). The Pope bluntly declared: "The world, in fact, needs Christ and it is the Church who must bring Christ to the world" through "the duty of the ministry and of the spiritual guidance of the Apostolic See, which is raised above the fate of the whole of mankind" (radio address, September 11, 1962). In keeping with his deep awareness of the primacy of the Church the Pope, from beginning to end, held fast to the theme of the Church's ability to establish unity, concord and peace on the foundation of truth. Whereas the unity of leadership was at first solidly structured along more hierarchical lines— "just as the faithful are subordinated to priests, and priests to bishops, so are all the individual bishops subordinated to the Roman Pontiff"—the council later appears as "the brotherly gathering of the bishops." Meanwhile, in the practical order, the Pope had transformed the curial concept of primacy into the evangelical form of his brotherly feelings (Christmas Address 1962). The encyclical Mater et Magistra was also conceived in terms of the obligation of the Church to promote love and good feelings.

Among the theological particularities some traditional emphases require mention in this context, in addition to the obviously desired restraining of mariological tendencies. The latter were in no wise reinforced by the pilgrimage to Loreto on October 4, 1962 and by the childlike bearing toward the "Mater Dei et mater nostra" repeatedly and fervently professed publicly by the Pope. These emphases are: the renewal on April 2, 1959 of the 1949 decree of the Holy Office forbidding Catholics to support Communism and rejecting any pseudo-peace with Communism, a renewal strongly qualified later by the Pope's attitude toward the East in the last weeks just before the beginning of the Second Vatican Council; the monitum of the Holy Office, dated June 20, 1961, urging prudence in New Testament exegesis, demonstratively qualified later by the appointment of the rector of the Pontifical Biblical Institute, which was the target of this censure, to the preparatory conciliar commission on theology. This monitum was even further qualified on November 20, 1962 when the Pope intervened to withdraw the schema on revelation. The Apostolic Constitution Veterum sapientia, devoted to the promotion of Latin and describing it as the "the unchangeable language" which possessed great advantages for maintaining the purity of revelation (February 22, 1962), was followed by the attempt to find "different forms and attitudes for the external transmission and frame of the living substance of doctrinal legacy" or, in other words, to dispense with historically conditioned formulations in the interests of pastoral care (see "Christian Unity"). Finally the monitum of the Holy Office, dated June 30, 1962, together with the official commentary that appeared in L'Osservatore Romano (June 30–July 1, 1962), which dealt with the dangers involved in the theological interpretation of the works of Teilhard de Chardin, preserved dogma from impermissable "transpositions."

2. Pope John's Church-consciousness in liturgical matters was directly evidenced during his celebration of Holy Week in St. Peter's Church in 1959. Here the Pope (for the first time in ninety years) publicly performed the ceremony of washing the feet of young priests, thereby symbolically laying aside all the signs of his pontifical dignity. In the Good Friday prayers he altered the prayer "pro perfidis Judaeis" to "pro Judaeis." As the Bishop of Rome he was present among his flock in all the liturgical celebrations of Holy Week. The Pope also deleted the offending allusion to Islam and to the "formerly chosen people" (July 18, 1959) in the consecration prayer to Christ the King. And the Apostolic Brief on the veneration of the Precious Blood of Jesus (June 30, 1960) essentially served the purpose of deepening biblical understanding of the redemptive work of Jesus. The Pope had expressed his approval of the use of vernacular languages in the liturgy long before the council, in a decision forwarded to Maximos IV Saigh on March 31, 1960. An Apostolic Brief, dated March 19, 1961, paved the way for the inclusion of St. Joseph in the Canon of the

Mass. A Brief celebrating the fiftieth anniversary of the Pontifical Institute of Sacred Music hailed the cultivation of Latin in the *liturgia solemnis*. At the same time however it expressed a desire for a better form of liturgical religious instruction and for a greater use of liturgical devotional books. During the first week of the council, at the daily Mass celebrated in the aula of the council, the Pope honored the different rites as a sign of unity and catholicity (Coronation Day Address, November 4, 1962).

The provisional reform of the rubrics in the Roman Breviary and missal, ushered in with the Motu proprio of July 25, 1960, is the most comprehensive of the liturgical documents. This reform extends of course only to parts of the Breviary. In addition to being a codification of the decrees of former Popes it constitutes an abridgment and a kind of unification of the Breviary involving no fundamental changes. It is of great usefulness to pastors, imposing no minimum requirements on them as regards official prayer. This work of abridgment and unification was probably more in keeping with an attempt on the part of the Curia to forestall the council than with the Pope's wishes, thereby engendering uncertainty among the clergy. The decree of the Holy Office, dated March 21, 1960, allowing the faithful to receive communion in the late afternoon or at night even without the previous celebration of Mass, shows to what extent the Church, urged on by the Pope, opens the way for the faithful to a sanctified togetherness with Christ.

3. Pope John was most strongly in his element in connection with his efforts to deepen the priestly life of the secular

clergy and of the religious in orders. The Pope gave practical instructions on proclaiming the word of God which he so desired to see applied, and which he himself practiced, in his address on February 10, 1959 to the Roman Lenten preachers: solid preparation and instruction, simplicity and above all love pouring forth from humble hearts, which alone can convince: "Speak exactly the same way that Jesus spoke to the people!"

The encyclical *Sacerdotii nostri primordia*, promulgated on the centenary of the death of the saintly Curé of Ars (August 1, 1959), constituted the core of this papal directive. It was a continuation of the ideas expressed by Pius XII in *Menti nostrae*: the example of evangelical poverty as the surest antidote to the mania of the faithful for material well-being; also obedience to ecclesiastical authority, devotion to the Eucharist, tireless pastoral zeal, above all the wisdom of the Cross and the representative penance for sinners. In this sense the Pope, discussing the education of candidates for the priesthood, expressed opposition "to the guidelines of modern pedagogical tendencies that are not always acceptable." Hence the precise and strict requirements promulgated on February 2, 1961 by the Sacred Congregation of Religious regarding the training and selection of candidates for the orders and the secular clergy. This promulgation also explains why a circular of the Sacred Congregation of Seminaries and Universities opposed as irresponsible the ordination "even of mediocre priest-candidates." A Brief of John XXIII addressed to religious orders for women (July 2, 1962) placed them in the service of the council. He admonished them against the "heresy of action" and exhorted

them always to nourish prayer "from the source of Holy
Scripture, above all from the New Testament, as well as
from the liturgy and the teaching of the Church in her
whole fullness." For all the remonstrances of Cardinal
Feltin the decision of the Holy Office, dated July 3, 1959, to
replace the French worker-priests by lay persons was a decision—as we now know today—which is to be understood
in terms of the renewal of the whole Church and of her
efforts to participate in the guidance of the world's destiny.

Sources

1. Christmas Message 1958, AAS 1958, 5–15; Christmas Message
1959, AAS 1960, 27–35; Apostolic Brief Quotiescumque to Cardinal Tien Chen-sin, June 29, 1961, AAS 1961, 465–469; encyclical
Ad Petri cathedram, AAS 1959, 497–531; Epistula Mirabilis ille to
the bishops, January 6, 1963; Pentecost homily 1962, AAS 1962,
437–447; encyclical Aeterna Dei, AAS 1961, 785–803; radio message, September 11, 1962, AAS 1962, 678–685; Christmas Message
1962, AAS 1963, 13–19; encyclical Mater et Magistra, AAS 1961,
401–461; decree dated April 4, 1959 on the political elections, AAS
1959, 271–272; "Against a pseudo-peace," general prayer intention
for August 1961; monitum on the exegesis of the New Testament,
AAS 1961, 507; Apostolic Constitution Veterum sapienta, AAS
1962, 129–135; address on the first anniversary of his coronation,
November 4, 1962, AAS 1962, 851–859; monitum concerning Teilhard de Chardin, June 30, 1962, AAS 1962, 526.

2. Alteration of the consecration prayer to Christ the King, July 18,
1959, AAS 1959, 595–596; Apostolic Brief Inde a primis on the
veneration of the Precious Blood, AAS 1960, 545–550; Brief to Patriarch Maximos IV Saigh, March 31, 1960; Apostolic Circular Le
voci on St. Joseph, AAS 1961, 205–213; Circular Iucunda laudatio
to the Papal Institute for Church Music, December 8, 1961, AAS
1961, 810–813; address on the first anniversary of his coronation,

November 4, 1962, *AAS* 1962, 851–859; Motu proprio *Rubricarum instructum*, *AAS* 1960, 593–595; decree on the evening reception of communion, March 21, 1960, *AAS* 1960, 355–356.

3. Address to the Lenten preachers of Rome, on February 10, 1959, *AAS* 1959, 190–195; encyclical *Sacerdotii nostri primordia*, *AAS* 1959, 545–579; address to candidates for the priesthood for Italy; Circular of the Congregation of Seminaries and Universities on the principles for the selection and training of candidates for the priesthood; Brief to religious orders for women, July 2, 1962, *AAS* 1962, 508–517; decree on worker-priests, July 3, 1959.

The Pastoral Teaching Office

1. The pastoral element emerged more strongly than the dogmatic in the teaching office of John XXIII. This is evidenced by the many impromptu addresses that were not published verbatim, not even in *L'Osservatore Romano*. Nor are they contained in the *Acta Apostolicae Sedis*. Although it would not be possible to document this assertion in detail, seemingly the Holy Father never missed an available opportunity to address a pastoral word to a person, or a group of persons, whom he happened to meet. He spoke to them extemporaneously, just as the words came to his heart and mind. The content of his utterances on such occasions, *"parole di circostanza"* as the Italians say, reflected simple thoughts and ideas whose impact on listeners derived from the Pope's personality. But they were utterances which he had a supreme gift for expressing at precisely the right moment. Such utterances are naturally outside the scope of a documentation of this kind.

2. The encyclicals *Ad Petri cathedram*, *Grata recordatio*, *Princeps pastorum* and *Paenitentiam agere* especially bear the marks of Pope John's preoccupation with pastoral care. In his inaugural encyclical the Pope exhorted the faithful to open their hearts to the truth: "Let us fulfill the truth in

love and we will grow in Him, our Lord, Jesus Christ." As
he uttered these words it was the press, radio, film and TV,
which today can search out the path to truth in all areas of
life, that immediately came to his mind. Already at that time
Pope John envisioned truth in the service of peace, of unity
and of harmony between persons, social strata and classes,
as well as between nations. In the famous words pronounced by the Pope in this context: "God did not create
men as enemies, but as brothers," it was again the universal
shepherd speaking. The pastoral note was also struck in his
ardent, obviously heartfelt wish "that all may be one," to
which the third part of the encyclical is devoted. The Pope
further declared: "This sweet hope has encouraged us publicly to proclaim our intention of convoking an ecumenical
council." Pope John considered the aggiornamento of the
Church, i.e. the adaptation of the Church to the conditions
of the modern world, as a first step in the direction of unity.

The encyclical *Grata recordatio* on the devotion to the
rosary in a way recalls Pius V, who had hoped to halt the in-
cursion of the Turks into Europe by praying the rosary.
John XXIII likewise named his intentions in this circular:
missionary activity and peace. In his view these are the
graces that the Mother of God can grant our era. In the
encyclical specifically dealing with missions, *Princeps pastorum,* he returned to the problem of missionary work,
which he had already described as his major concern, dealing with it along the lines of "*omnes unum sint,*" "that all
may be one."

The circular *Paenitentiam agere* constitutes one of the
most important documents of Pope John's pastoral doc-

trine. He wanted the penance of the faithful to prepare the way for the ecumenical council because every work of an ecclesiastical and Christian character begins with an expression of penance. Here Pope John elucidated the significance and the forms of penitence in a way that makes this document an eminently useful one to consult for a discussion of this theme.

3. Much of Pope John's pastoral teaching was contained in the radio messages that he delivered to the world on high feast days. Here we will list only the major concerns of these messages: next to ideas revolving around the subject of Christian unity, which resound in almost all these messages, the peace theme increasingly assumed greater prominence from year to year. Both concerns were closely linked. Unity is the prerequisite of true peace in justice and brotherhood, the latter appearing as the fruit of unity. In the course of the pontificate this leitmotif of his pastoral care was also instrumental in broadening the circle of people for whom the Pope felt a deep sense of responsibility. This found its most notable expression in his opening address to the council, during which he declared that the unity which Jesus Christ had given to his Church radiated in a threefold light: as the "unity of Catholics among themselves, which must be solidly preserved as an illuminating example," as a "unity which exists in the prayer and in the ardent expectations of Christians separated from the Apostolic See," and finally as the "unity of the esteem and reverence which is shown the Catholic Church by other religions which are not yet Christian." Pope John also saw therein the radiance of divine

grace and a beginning of the realization of the great goal of unity.

It is hardly surprising that in addition to these concerns Pope John, often called the *"parroco del mondo"* "pastor of the world," should also evince a deep concern for the personal salvation of the faithful in his addresses to them as a body. Thus in his Easter allocution in 1959 he called upon the faithful not to forget the Easter sacrament. Pope John concluded this portion of the allocution with the words: "The Lord is truly risen! We must also be able to say this of every single one of our brothers: he who was in sin is truly risen. The doubting, the mistrustful, the fearful, the lukewarm have risen! The careworn, the suffering, the afflicted, the wretched have risen! This is the wish that we offer you, beloved children, in the fatherly love of our heart! Your life is sheltered in God with Christ!"

Pope John delivered a homily on the occasion of the first anniversary of his coronation. In it he recalled that on the day of his election he had urged "souls to recite the divine prayer of the Our Father" because it contains "the most essential things" for which we must petition him and which are given to us.

The Pope struck a wholly pastoral note in his 1960 Christmas Message: "We must confess to you that our reflection feels drawn above all to the truth, and all the more so since the experience of pastoral life provides ever clearer examples of this which is especially important and needful of being deepened." This meditation was followed by the call to live in truth along the lines of a fourfold truth: to think, to honor, to speak and to act out the truth. "Beloved sons! No!

Never lend yourselves to the falsification of truth! Shun this with a sense of horror. Grace and truth, this is the quintessence of that which the Son of God has brought us through his incarnation." This Christmas Message was one of the most stirring sermons ever delivered by Pope John.

A triumphant note of optimism always marked the Pope's Easter messages. This no doubt was a characteristic feature of the late Pope's personality and it can most aptly be summed up with the simple phrase "trust in God." Even when an Easter Message, like that of 1961, dealt primarily with his concern over the tribulations of the Church it nevertheless struck a note of supreme confidence: Christ is the resurrection and the life, and we must consider our own personal and social life in terms of this point of view.

The "simple son of the people" who had been called to the governance of the Church—even this personal note belonged to the "pastoral" theme—placed himself "for the fourth time in the service of the great message of peace" on Christmas Day, 1961. But this time he did so in order to describe the kingdom of Christ as the kingdom of goodness, and peace as the fruit of goodness. Upon reading the messages we are struck by the frequency and the impressiveness with which Pope John described the mercy of God and of his son, Jesus Christ. This Christmas Message contains the memorable words: "To lament over evil is saddening. Yet we know that lamentations alone will not conquer evil . . . Goodness must be proclaimed."

The Easter Message in 1962 also began with a personal reminiscence. This time the Pope recalled Bulgaria and the "many kind and delightful persons whom we met there."

The message continued with a profession of his dedication to the loftiest task of the apostolic office, which endows the holder with its authentic character in accordance with the will of the Lord. "The care of souls that is expressed through our words and every other activity of our office aims to bear witness to the resurrection of Jesus!" The *"Khristos Woskress"* with which the Slavic liturgies express their Easter joy seemed to him the most perfect and fullest expression of the confession of faith. Because our Lord Jesus is risen, faith prevails over history. As the Pope said on this occasion the council too should become a new Easter and Pentecost for the Church. He returned to these themes in the Pentecost homily of the same year. The mission of our lives, of the life of the Church, especially also of the council then in the offing are to bear witness to Christ, the Lord and Master, the Shepherd and the Priest, the sacrificial Victim of mankind.

A reading of the last two festive messages of the Holy Father, delivered on Christmas Day, 1962 and on Easter Sunday, 1963, engender an emotion of a special kind. In the Christmas Message Pope John reviewed the work of the council which had just concluded its first session: "The most characteristic event of the ecumenical council was the spontaneous flowering of the desire for unity, which almost no one expected. It would be better to say of the desire for a deliberate, acknowledged and highly welcome orientation of Christian brotherhood . . . of a Church that exists not to wield dominion over peoples but to serve them and for whom Christ's plan is a goal for which she honorably strives." Thereupon he dedicated himself to achieving the goal of unity with deeply stirring words. The Easter Message ended with the prayer: "*Agnus Dei, qui tollis paccata mundi, dona nobis pacem* . . . so that peace, your peace, will reign in hearts, in families and in the world."

4. As part of the duties inherent in the nature of the papal office the Holy Father was constantly granting audiences: to the countless groups of pilgrims arriving in Rome, to the faithful who lived in the Eternal City itself, to participants in international events, such as the Olympics, or to persons attending the various congresses and conventions being held in the city. The manner with which he received them and the words which he spoke to them also mirror the lineaments of Pope John's personality as a universal shepherd. But we refer to them here only in passing.

Already in his first encyclical Pope John had devoted the last, and relatively most comprehensive, part of his exhortation to the different social strata and classes of persons, especially the oppressed, the careworn, the needy, the refugees, the emigrants and the victims of religious persecution. In his last Christmas Message, marked by a warm-heartedness peculiarly his own, Pope John identified himself with all those upon whom the pastor's special care must be bestowed: on families and their dwellings, on the poor, the workers, on those engaged in scientific activity, the suffering, the aged, the children, the young, on fathers and mothers. He called to them in the words of Augustine: "Let us enkindle love!" and turned prayerfully to the Lord, the Son of God and Mary, beseeching him to clothe with immortality, to inflame with love and to unite all the children of his redemption through the bonds of his Mystical Body.

5. Two occupational groups were made to feel that the Pope considered himself especially bound to them. These were the workers—actually it would be more correct to say the producers because he never forgot the intellectual workers—and journalists and publicists of all kinds.

One event stands out as being most characteristic of the special worth Pope John placed on labor. On November 25, 1961, through the Sacred Apostolic Penitentiary, he granted a plenary indulgence—under the usual conditions—to those who every morning in one form or other expressly offer up their work to God, whether it be work of hand or mind. This plenary indulgence was instituted "so that human labor by dedicating itself to God may be all the more ennobled and related to things religious." Although this decree and the reasons underlying it are important in themselves, not to mention Pope John's understanding of the work-obsessed man of our day, too little attention has been paid to this indulgence and it has not been accorded the full appraisal that is its due.

Pope John delivered one of his first addresses to an occupational group to the Christian Employers Association of Italy. This address contained the statement that must always be taken into consideration in connection with the totality of his utterances dealing with social questions: "The Pope's teaching on social cooperation and activity receives its light from the gospel." It does not bear the stamp of a socio-philosophical doctrine but that of a pastoral approach. Even at that time he was exhorting employers and executives to work not only for the social welfare but also for the higher goods that await us all, laying special emphasis in his exhortation on understanding.

He addressed workers in a similar vein on May Day, 1959: "You should know that the Pope is with you." He told them how the workers had won his affection when as a young priest he had been secretary to the social-minded Bishop Giacomo Radini-Tedeschi. Immediately thereafter he guided their thoughts to their apostolic duty as regards their fellow-workers who need "love and understanding" because their faith has been shaken. The address concluded with a fervent supplication to St. Joseph the Worker. One year later he again set the Holy Family of Nazareth in the center of his discussion of the significance of work in human life, viewing work wholly in terms of the gospel. He also used the gospel as a standard for judging the false ideologies concerning the nature of work and workers that are being propagated in our day. What is supremely necessary, declared Pope John, is to spread the teaching and the peace of Christ among the working classes.

6. The Pope viewed journalists as his special allies. Indeed he counted them as among his most important collaborators in the struggle for world peace and unity. He held all journalists in high esteem whether or not they were Catholics, whether they wrote for newspapers or periodicals or were engaged in radio or TV journalism. This esteem was most fully expressed in his speech of December 4, 1960 wherein he pointed out that the journalist "must possess the sensitivity of a physician, the versatility of an author, the circumspection of a jurist and the feeling of responsibility of an educator." Moreover the Pope often complimented journalists for the fact that they actually possessed these attributes.

In his talks with journalists he especially emphasized that in their hearts they should remain loyal to truth, viewed as the foundation of all social existence. Further he exhorted them to foster unity and harmony among peoples, especially among Catholics, and to let themselves be guided by this "Christian feeling" which is mindful of the commandment of love above all. At the same time he often went into details, thereby also showing his own interest in the workings of the press. He warned against futile polemics as well as against an inopportune readiness for unprincipled compromise and accommodation. Pope John pleaded for argumentations instead of phrase-mongering, evincing a great distress over all sycophantic glorification, especially with respect to living persons, and over the indiscretion and tactlessness that so often is the hallmark of contemporary journalism. "Veritatem in caritate!" was his exhortation to sportswriters on April 2, 1960. On October 24, 1961 Pope John gave news correspondents in Rome the "friendly advice" to place all their energies in the service of truth. He told them that by so doing they would automatically be active in the promotion of world brotherhood. Further he praised them for the rising level of religious reporting, evidenced even by neutral newspapers. Pope John delivered his last exhortation on the responsibility of Catholic publicists—it was also the last time he praised them because in general they had successfully discharged their duty—on January 27, 1963 during his audience with the members of the editorial staff of the L'Osservatore Romano and the Catholic journalists who accompanied them.

7. Teachers were another occupational group with whom Pope John felt a special bond of sympathy and interest. Bypassing the numerous briefer addresses he made to teachers and educators, we will recall here the promise that the Pope made in his address of September 6, 1959: "We should like to confide a final thought to you which we hope may also comfort you in carrying out the duties previously mentioned. As you unfold the mind of your pupils and form their souls, you are preparing for yourselves one of the most magnificent crowns among those of heaven." Thereupon the Pope quoted John Chrysostom, who set the influence of education high above that of all the other arts.

8. Practically all of the most important documents of Pope John's pastoral teaching office bear witness to the fact that the family constituted a special object of Pope John's pastoral care. Here we will mention only two of these documents: in his address to Italian women on March 1, 1959 the Pope sang a hymn of praise to Christian motherhood and to its quintessence, love. Here too remembrance of his childhood served as a point of departure. Discussing his attitude toward the employment of women in industry, the Pope recognized the fact that today it is often necessary for women to work and that it can be highly valuable. Nevertheless the specific mission of women lies in motherhood unless they have a vocation for the religious life. He discussed this theme in greater detail in his address to the Roman Rota on October 25, 1960, wherein he touched upon "the very great problem of the sacredness of marriage" and stressed the necessity of the "solidity of doctrine." This speech was impressive evidence of the Holy Father's great care to preserve and safeguard apostolic teaching, even in the exercise of his pastoral office. It clearly shows how little he was disposed to compromise on this point. But even this address concluded with the remark that he merely wanted to express "some ideas of a pastoral character."

9. Finally in the framework of Pope John's pastoral teaching we must recall the support that he joyfully extended to all the works and all the groups connected with Catholic Action. Catholic Action had been close to his heart ever since his youth. As Patriarch of Venice it had once been his intention to publish a long pastoral letter on the subject of Catholic Action. This plan was not realized at that time, nor was it realized after he became Pope, even though by his own statement he had once again expressly set himself this task. Thus all that remains for us are his pastoral exhortations. We will discuss the encyclical *Princeps pastorum* elsewhere in connection with its teaching on the cooperation of the laity in the work of the missions.

The Pope outlined ways in which lay persons can cooperate with the hierarchical apostolate of the Church in his address of January 10, 1960 to an audience of young women, and in his address of May 13, 1962 to a group of Italian men. Such cooperation must be carried out in full obedience to the hierarchy. This very subordination to the hierarchy constitutes the feature that distinguishes this cooperation from that prevailing in other Christian-religious or Christian-secular organizations. The aim of Catholic Action consists in the effort to transform into reality the petition "Thy kingdom come" contained in the Our Father. It is a

social aim focused on the edification and consolidation of
the Church and on the redemption of individual souls.

It necessarily follows therefrom that every member must
lead a fervent religious life. Here is said to lie the mystery
of the fruitfulness of every apostolic work: it is said to
depend on the earnestness with which we take the "primacy
of the supernatural" in the order of things. These addresses
too echoed the Pope's leitmotif when he concluded them
by hailing the Catholic Action movement as a bearer of
light and of peace.

Sources

2. Encyclical *Ad Petri cathedram*, AAS 1959, 497–531; encyclical
Grata recordatio, AAS 1959, 673–678; encyclical *Princeps pastorum*,
AAS 1959, 833–864; encyclical *Paenitentiam agere*, AAS 1962,
481–491.

3. Christmas Message 1958, AAS 1959, 5–12; Easter Message 1959,
AAS 1959, 241–255; Easter homily 1959, AAS 1959, 245–252;
homily on the first anniversary of his coronation, AAS 1959, 814–
818; Christmas Message 1959, AAS 1960, 27–35, Easter Message
1960, AAS 1960, 369–371; Pentecost Message 1960, AAS 1960,
517–526; Christmas Message 1960, AAS 1961, 5–15; address on the
anniversary of his coronation, 1961, AAS 1962, 14–22; Easter Message 1962, AAS 1962, 291–295; Pentecost homily 1962, AAS 1962,
437–447; homily on the anniversary of his coronation 1962, AAS
1962, 851–859; Christmas Message 1962, AAS 1963, 13–19; Easter
Message 1963.

4. Address on the Olympic Games, August 28 and 29, 1960, AAS
1960, 817–821.

5. Decree of the Apostolic Penitentiary, November 25, 1961, AAS
1961, 827; address to the Christian Employers Association of Italy,
January 30, 1959, AAS 1959, 80–81; message to the working class,

May 1, 1959, *AAS* 1959, 355–359; address to the Congress for the Humanization of Labor, October 17, 1959, *AAS* 1959, 821–822; message to the working class, May 1, 1960, *AAS* 1960, 397–400.

6. Address to journalists, May 4, 1959, *AAS* 1959, 359–362; on October 24, 1961, *AAS* 1961, 721–724; on May 28, 1962, *AAS* 1962, 455–457; on October 13, 1962, *AAS* 1962, 816–819; on January 27, 1963, *AAS* 1963, 99–105; address to the Association of Italian Jurists, December 8, 1959, *AAS* 1960, 45–50.

7. Address to Italian Catholic Teachers, September 6, 1959, *AAS* 1959, 703–706; address to Teaching Brothers, June 14, 1961.

8. Address to Italian Catholic Women, March 1, 1959, *AAS* 1959, 195–197; to the Roman Rota, October 25, 1960, *AAS* 1960, 898–903; on women's work, see address of April 24, 1960, *AAS* 1960, 390–393 and that of September 6, 1961, *AAS* 1961, 610–612.

9. Encyclical *Ad Petri Cathedram*, *AAS* 1959, 497–531; *Princeps pastorum*, *AAS* 1959, 833–864; address of January 10, 1960, *AAS* 1960, 83–90; addresses of December 10, 1961, December 12, 1961 and January 5, 1962; Address of May 13, 1962, *AAS* 1962, 400–404.

The Governance of the Church

1. In the homily delivered at his coronation Mass Pope John said that he wished above all to be a good shepherd. This intention found its most consistent and overt expression in our time in the convocation and opening of the Second Vatican Council. This council was the greatest achievement of his pontificate. The convocation of the Roman diocesan synod, held from January 24 to 31, 1960, can be called his second greatest achievement. Obviously it was a governmental act on the part of the Bishop of Rome. But as Ireneus already said long ago (*Adv. Haere* III, 3, 2) "every Church must be in agreement with this Church because of her special primacy." Although this agreement should not be interpreted in the sense of a total uniformity, the way in which the Pope administers the bishopric of Rome is a beacon light for the whole Church. Thus the diocesan synod must be recalled here at least once again. Pope John could realize only the beginnings of the third great goal of his pontificate, the revision of canon law. He appointed the members of the commission who were to tackle this problem at the beginning of April 1963.

2. If we disregard these extraordinary acts, or plans, of Pope John's governance of the Church, then a whole series of canonical decisions relating to Church polity—which in part will be dealt with elsewhere—must be viewed as events and accomplishments produced by the routine exercise of the highest pastoral office. Yet it must be recalled beforehand, and precisely so with many of Pope John's measures, that he tried to gauge all his decisions in the guiding light of his conception of the duties devolving upon the good shepherd.

Transmission of the truth seemed to him the loftiest task entrusted to the pastor of the universal Church. "The highest honor of every pontificate really lies in the practical consonance with the injunction of the gospel: 'Go forth and teach!'" Although the teaching that Pope John bequeathed us is presented separately, his eight encyclicals at least should be reckoned here as acts of his governance of the Church. They are: *Ad Petri cathedram*, dated June 29, 1959, promulgated at the beginning of his pontificate, and dealing with the themes of truth, unity, concord and peace, and also containing paternal admonitions to many groups of persons; *Sacerdotii nostri primordia*, dated August 1, 1959, on the saintly Curé of Ars; *Grata recordatio*, dated September 26, 1959, on the furtherance and fostering of devotion to the rosary; *Princeps pastorum*, dated November 28, 1959, on the work of the missions; *Mater et Magistra*, May 15, 1961, on the latest developments of social life and of its structuring in the light of Christian teaching; *Aeterna Dei*, dated November 11, 1961, celebrating St. Leo the Great on the fifteen hundredth anniversary of his death; *Paenitentiam agere*, dated July 1, 1962, containing the call to prepare for the council through penance; and finally *Pacem in terris*, dated April 11, 1963, which, so to speak, was Pope John's testament to all men of good will.

3. The pastoral office and the teaching office also accorded with one another in the beatifications and canonizations of saints. Both pursued the aim of providing the faithful with models of exemplary spirituality.

The following were canonized: the Franciscan Carolus a Setia and the Blessed Joachima de Vedruna, widowed de Mas, on April 12, 1959; Cardinal Gregorio Barbarigo (Gregorious Barbadicus) on May 26, 1960; the archbishop of Valencia Johannes de Ribera on June 12, 1960; the nun Maria Bertilla Boscardin on May 11, 1961; the Dominican Martino de Porres on May 6, 1962; the priest Peter Julian Eymard, the Servite Antonio Maria Pucci and the Capuchin brother Franciscus Maria a Camporubeo on December 9, 1962; and finally Vincent Pallotti, founder of the missionary society that bears his name, on January 20, 1963. On March 18, 1959 St. Laurentius of Brindisi was accorded the honor of being proclaimed a doctor of the Church.

The following were beatified: Helena Guerra, foundress of a sisterhood, on April 26, 1959; Maria Margarita Dufrost de Lajemmerais, widowed d'Youville, also the foundress of a sisterhood, on May 3, 1959; the Capuchin Innocentius a Bertio on November 12, 1961; Elizabeth Ann Bayley, widowed Seton, on March 17, 1963; and the priest Aloysius Maria Palazzolo on March 19, 1963.

4. The establishment of a regular native hierarchy in mission countries was one of the most important accomplishments of the Johannine pontificate.

Under John XXIII the hierarchy was established in the

Belgian Congo and Ruanda-Urundi on November 10, 1959; in the Bahama Islands on July 5, 1960; in Vietnam on November 24, 1960; in Indonesia on January 3, 1961; and in Korea on March 10, 1962. The Pope also established Apostolic Delegations in Scandinavia on March 1, 1960 and one each in East Africa, Madagascar, West Africa and Central West Africa on May 3, 1960.

5. The increased importance which the deceased Pontiff accorded the College of Cardinals as a real senate acting in close collaboration with the Pope was especially characteristic of Pope John's views regarding Church government. In his address to the secret consistory on March 19, 1962, he outlined his conception of the duties devolving upon the cardinals. The purple robe is not awarded to cardinals primarily as a reward for their services. Rather it places upon those who wear it the responsibility of expending all their energies in the service of the Holy See, with whom the College of Cardinals must now share the increasingly heavy burdens of guiding and administering the universal Church.

As Pope John acknowledged at that time, this was the reason he went beyond the number of seventy cardinals as is prescribed in canon 251. He elevated the following persons to the cardinalate: at the Consistory of December 15, 1951: 1. Giovanni Montini, Archbishop of Milan; 2. Giovanni Urbani, Patriarch of Venice; 3. Paolo Giobbe, Nuncio to The Netherlands; 4. Giuseppe Fietta, Nuncio to Italy; 5. Fernando Cento, Nuncio to Portugal; 6. Carlo Chiarlo, Nuncio at disposition of the Holy See; 7. Amleto J. Cicognani, Apostolic Delegate to the United States; 8. José Garibi y Rivera, Archbishop of Guadalajara, Mexico; 9. Antonio

Maria Barbieri, Archbishop of Montevideo; 10. William
Godfrey, Archbishop of Westminister; 11. Carlo Confa-
lonieri, Secretary of the Sacred Congregation of Studies; 12.
Richard J. Cushing, Archbishop of Boston; 13. Alfonso
Castaldo, Archbishop of Naples; 14. Paul Marie Richaud,
Archbishop of Bordeaux; 15. John O'Hara, Archbishop of
Philadelphia; 16. José M. Bueno y Monreal, Archbishop of
Sevilla; 17. Franz König, Archbishop of Vienna; 18. Julius
Döpfner, Bishop of Berlin; 19. Domenico Tardini, Secre-
tary of State; 20. Alberto di Jorio, general auditor of the
Apostolic Church; 21. Francesco Bracci, Secretary of the
Sacred Congregation of Sacraments; 22. Francesco Roberti,
Secretary of the Congregation of the Council; 23. André
Jullien, deacon of the Rota.

At the consistory of December 14, 1959: 1. Paolo Mar-
ella, Nuncio to France; 2. Gustavo Testa, Nuncio to Swit-
zerland; 3. Alois Joseph Muench, Nuncio to Germany; 4.
Albert Gregory Meyer, Archbishop of Chicago; 5. Arcadio
Larraona, Secretary of the Sacred Congregation of Rites; 6.
Francesco Morano, Secretary of the Apostolic Signitura; 7.
William Theodore Heard, deacon of the Rota; 8. Augustin
Bea S.J.

At the consistory of March 28, 1960: 1. Luigi Traglia,
Vicegerunt of Rome; 2. Petrus Tatsuo Doi, Archbishop of
Tokyo; 3. Joseph Lefebvre, Archbishop of Bourges; 4. Bern-
hard Johannes Alfrink, Archbishop of Utrecht; 5. Rufino I.
Santos, Archbishop of Manila; 6. Laurian Rugambwa, Arch-
bishop of Rutabo; 7. Antonio Bacci, Secretary of Briefs to
Princes.

At the consistory of January 16, 1961: 1. Joseph Ritter,

Archbishop of St. Louis; 2. José Quintero, Archbishop of Caracas; 3. Luis Concha Córdoba, Archbishop of Bogotá; 4. Giuseppe Ferretto, Secretary of the Sacred College of Cardinals.

At the consistory of March 19, 1962: 1. Joseph da Costa Núñez, Vice Chamberlain of the Church; 2. Giovanni Panico, Nuncio to Portugal; 3. Ildebrando Antoniutti, Nuncio to Spain; 4. Ephraim Forni, Nuncio to Belgium; 5. Juan Landázuri Ricketts, Archbishop of Lima; 6. Gabriel Coussa, Pro-Secretary of the Congregation for the Oriental Church; 7. Raul Silva Henríquez, Archbishop of Santiago; 8. Leo Suenens, Archbishop of Mecheln and Brussels; 9. Michael Browne, General of the Dominican Order; 10. Anselmo M. Albareda, Prefect of the Vatican Library.

Pope John appointed a great number of cardinals, if the additions to the cardinalate are measured against the duration of his pontificate. Among them are many resident bishops who represent Africa, Asia and America. Nevertheless the long list of curia cardinals is striking.

6. Pope John wanted to regenerate the Roman curia because he did not find it expedient to govern by himself. This was in keeping with his character. By so doing he reversed the procedure of his predecessors. Pius XII had allowed the number of his closest collaborators increasingly to shrink during the course of his pontificate. He had personally directed the Secretariat of State and had entrusted some of the few remaining curia cardinals with the presidency of several congregations and with the administration of a few offices. John XXIII, instead, gradually increased the number of cardinals so that eventually they exceeded the number of

cardinal offices. These were curia cardinals who could actually devote their activity exclusively to cooperation with the congregations and thus relieve their directors of their burdens. Pope John himself said that he was dependent not only on this cooperation, but above all on the advice of the members of the Sacred College.

The reestablishment of the so-called tabellar audiences with officials of the congregations and with the Secretariat of State, residing in Rome, and the reactivation of offices provided for in canon law belong among the first governmental acts instituted by John XXIII. On November 17, 1958 he appointed Monsignor Domenico Tardini Secretary of State and in his next consistory he elevated him to the rank of cardinal. Upon the latter's death, on August 12, 1961, he was succeeded by Cardinal Amleto Cicognani in a post that involves much close collaboration with the Holy Father. Pope John also reestablished the former structure of the Holy Office on October 23, 1959 by appointing the former Archbishop of Perugia, Pietro Parente, as assessor in the second highest post of this highest body among all the Roman congregations. Several days later, upon the retirement of Cardinal Pizzardo on November 7, 1959, he entrusted Cardinal Alfredo Ottaviani with the office of secretary of the Holy Office. The directorship of the Sacred Congregation for the Oriental Church also changed hands during these same days. Cardinal Tisserant resigned. On November 14, 1959 he was replaced by Cardinal Amleto Cicognani as secretary of this congregation whose top directorate, like that of the Holy Office, is personally subject to the Pope. After the latter had become Secretary of State he was succeeded, on August 13, 1961, by a member of the Oriental Church, Archbishop Gabriel Coussa, at first in the position of a Pro-Secretary, and later as Secretary after his elevation to the cardinalate. Unfortunately Archbishop Coussa, who was eminently suited for precisely this office, died on July 29, 1962. The Pope himself delivered the memorial address in St. Peter's Basilica, just as he had personally consecrated him bishop on April 16, 1961. On August 2, 1962 the Pope then appointed Cardinal Gustavo Testa Secretary; Cardinal Testa is still in office. On the other hand Cardinal State Secretary Cicognani held the office of President of the Commission on Correspondence of the Ecumenical Council up to the end, probably because the Holy Father wanted to keep close contact with this commission through his foremost collaborator. Further it is worthy of note that Pope John, on December 24, 1959, decreed that in the future the Roman congregations were to invite to their plenary sessions all the archbishops and bishops of the world who might be sojourning in Rome who are also members of the College of Cardinals. And on March 19, 1963 Pope John broke with all tradition and appointed the four then-reigning Eastern and Latin Patriarchs of Jerusalem regular members of these congregations. Customarily however only cardinals can be members of sacred congregations.

The regulations concerning seven suburban bishoprics of Rome must also be mentioned as measures designed to adjust the structures of the Church to the needs of the times. On March 10, 1961 Pope John abrogated the optional rights of the cardinals to these bishoprics, thereby replacing the principle of seniority by the principle of selection based on

special aptitudes. But even greater innovations were necessary in order to cope with the necessity for real episcopal
pastoral care in these dioceses of suburban Rome which had
enormously increased in population. Thus on April 11, 1962
John XXIII ordained that cardinal-bishops should be only
the titular occupants of their bishoprics. Henceforth these
bishoprics were to be administered in fact and *de jure* by
regular bishops. At the same time Pope John placed the
bishops of all these dioceses under the direction of the
cardinal-vicar of Rome in their own bishops' conference.

Such innovations may be viewed as a model case of how,
on the one hand, Pope John wanted to claim the curia
cardinals wholly for the administration of the universal
Church. On the other hand they also show how desirous he
was that the latter conduct a satisfactory and truly func-
tional episcopal pastoral activity in their own bishoprics and
in their own Church province in conjunction with the
bishops of a sociologically defined region. Thus he appointed several suffragan bishops even for the bishopric of
Rome itself and elevated the Vicegerunt Traglia to the
cardinalate. As the last of his measures to increase the importance and effectiveness of the Sacred College we can also
cite his decree of April 15, 1962 which ordained that henceforth all cardinals are to possess the dignity of the status of
bishop. He himself imparted the episcopal consecration, on
Maundy Thursday 1962 in St. Peter's, to the cardinal dea-
cons, who had never attained this dignity hitherto in the
history of the Church.

7. The council has shown, as no document can, what a high
valuation the deceased Pope set on the office of the bishop.

He was fond of addressing the bishops as his brothers, a greeting with which he opened the council. He viewed himself as one among the episcopate and he combined his responsibility for the pastoral administration of the Church with that of the bishops, as a body. This joint character is especially evidenced in the Brief which the Holy Father addressed to the bishops on April 15, 1962 in which he requested them to prepare themselves for the council. In this communication, as the supreme head of the episcopate, he exhorted his episcopal colleagues to be ever mindful of the responsibility which the office of bishop lays upon its bearers. But he did not send this Brief to the episcopate of the whole world as a body, as was customary, but to each individual bishop personally in order, as he himself wrote, to give evidence of his friendly bond and devotion to each one. There are also other very cordial Briefs which the Pope sent to individual bishops which deviate from the official style. Let us also recall, as another example, the stirring and heartfelt reception that he accorded Cardinal Wyszynski.

But even more important seems to be the way in which the Pope, as Bishop of Rome, strove by example to show his colleagues that the most important part of the pastoral office does not lie in regulations of governance but in direct contact between pastor and parishioners. Immediately upon assuming office the Pope began, literally, to attend to his flock to an extent hitherto entirely unknown. He visited hospitals and orphanages, the Roman prison, above all a great number of parishes in the outskirts. Moreover he took part in religious services at the stational churches during the Lenten season, and never without addressing a fatherly

word of admonition to the faithful present. Also worthy of
mention is the fact that he ordered a wage increase for Vatican employees and workers, and the opening of the Vatican
gardens which formerly had been hermetically sealed off.
Rome understood and loved its Bishop. This was shown in
the days when a band of mourners swelled to millions who
came to bid final farewell to the deceased Pontiff when the
news of his death spread throughout the city.

8. The care and attention that the Pope extended to priests
and candidates for the priesthood was also related to his approach to the governance of the Church. In the encyclical
Sacerdotii nostri primordia and in the allocution to the
Roman clergy on November 24, 1960, when the synodal
decrees went into effect, the Pope pointed out to them the
duty of counseling, of exhorting, and above all of understanding the nature of priestly compassion. There is a
special tone of warmth in the talk he delivered on his visitations to various institutes for the training of priests shortly
after his coronation, for example on November 27, 1958 to
the Lateran Atheneum, on November 30 to the College of
the Propagation of the Faith, on January 18, 1959 to the
Gregorian Institute, on October 11, 1959 to the North
American College, on October 13 to the Anima. He raised
three of the Roman institutes to the status of university: the
Lateran University on May 17, 1959, the College of the
Propagation of the Faith on October 1, 1962 and the Angelicum of the Dominicans on March 7, 1963. Here it must be
mentioned that he also increased the number of Catholic
universities of a general character by three: Buenos Aires on
June 16, 1960, Navarra on October 6, 1960 and Vlaparaiso on

November 1, 1961. The Holy Father's attitude toward theological science, insofar as it is binding in a disciplinary sense, was expressed in the two *monita* of the Holy Office. The first, dated June 20, 1961, warned against minimalism in exegesis especially regarding the historicity of the bible; the second, dated June 30, 1962, warned against certain conceptions set forth by Teilhard de Chardin. But here reference should also be made to the eulogy which the Holy Father delivered on February 17, 1960 to the Pontifical Biblical Institute on the occasion of its fiftieth anniversary. This Institute, as is known, had been accused of rationalism in the last few years. Further, the Pope entrusted Father Augustin Bea, the *Spiritus rector* of the Biblical Institute for many years, with one of the most important tasks which he saw facing the Church today. Finally, in connection with the training of priests, mention must be made of the Pope's espousal of the Latin language as an instrument of theology. He devoted the Apostolic Constitution *Veterum sapientia*, February 22, 1962, to these concerns.

9. The regulation of relations between the Church, especially the Holy Office, and secular governments also belongs to the sphere of Church governance. The appeals of his teaching office are presented individually on 90 ff. Here it is a question of cultivating contact which is a prerequisite for the efficacy of the teaching office.

Today the Church enjoys diplomatic relations with states as never before. Historically this is traceable to the efforts of Pius XI and Pius XII in this direction. John XXIII added the finishing touches to this network of diplomatic relationships. The establishment of an internunciature in Turkey with its headquarters in Constantinople, which he was able to undertake on February 29, 1960, was a source of special joy to him. An internunciature was also established in Senegal on November 17, 1961 and two nuntiatures each in Burundi on February 11, 1963 and in Congo-Leopoldville on February 16, 1963.

10. Official state visits are a sign of our times. We no longer set a high value on them because they have become so numerous. Nevertheless we may trust politicians on this score. They appreciate their importance and for this very reason they cultivate and foster personal encounters. The same applies to visits that are made by the supreme heads of state. Hence we shall list here the visits that were made by the heads of state to the Pope. During his pontificate Pope John XXIII received the following heads of state: Shah of Persia Mohammed Riza Pahlevi (December 1, 1958), President Gronchi of Italy (May 6, 1959), President Sukarno of Indonesia (May 14, 1959), King Hussein I of Jordan (April 30, 1959), the *Capitani Reggenti* of San Marino (May 18, 1959), King Paul and Queen Frederika of Greece (May 22, 1959), President Bayer of Turkey (June 11, 1959), Prince Rainier and Princess Grace of Monaco (June 18 and November 7, 1959), President de Gaulle of France (June 27, 1959), President Bourgiba of Tunis (July 19, 1959), King Frederick IX and Queen Ingrid of Denmark (November 10, 1959), President Eisenhower (December 6, 1959), President Prado of Peru (February 22, 1960), President Frondizi of Argentina (June 18, 1960), King Bhumibol and Queen Sirikit of Thailand (October 1, 1960), Prince Franz Joseph II of Liechtenstein (October 8, 1960), King Gustav VI,

Adolph and Queen Louise of Sweden (October 31, 1960), President Nardone of Uruguay (December 3, 1960), Queen Elizabeth of Great Britain and Prince Philip (May 5, 1961), King Baudouin and Queen Fabiola of Belgium (June 8, 1961), President Yameogo of Upper Volta (April 25, 1962), President de Valera of Ireland (March 7, 1962), President Orlich of Costa Rica (March 18, 1962), newly elected Italian President Segni (July 3, 1962), President Macapagal of The Philippines (July 9, 1962), President Maga of Dahomey (September 25, 1962), President Sedar Senghor of Senegal (October 5, 1962), and King Mwambutsa IV of Burundi (December 16, 1962). The death of the Pope prevented the visit of the late President of the United States, John F. Kennedy, which had already been announced. In addition the Pope received many heads of government and ministers. Here we mention only the visit of Chancellor Adenauer and Chancellor Raab.

The messages which the Pope sent to the so-called underdeveloped countries when they achieved full national sovereignty also belong to the category of acts bearing a political character. They were of course sent to the competent bishops but they also were intended for the peoples themselves.

The *Acta Apostolicae Sedis* lists friendship greetings and blessings which were sent to the peoples of Togo (April 13, 1960), Congo-Leopoldville (June 30, 1960), Congo-Brazzaville (November 7, 1960), Upper Volta (December 10, 1961) and Nigeria (December 18, 1961).

Finally mention must be made of the state treaties entered into with Austria. The first, signed June 23, 1960, regulated financial questions; the second, signed July 9, 1962, dealt with the establishment of the bishopric of Eisenstadt and with the school question.

11. The question over which judgments on the pontificate of John XXIII tend to fluctuate strongly is that concerning his policy toward the governments of the Eastern bloc. This question would surely have found a definite answer had the Holy Father lived longer. Nevertheless the pronouncements he made or did not make on this subject, and individual actions such as the reception accorded to Khrushchev's son-in-law in the spring of 1963 and, perhaps, also the sending of Cardinal König and an official of the Secretariat of State to Budapest justify the assertion that the Pope was looking for a more flexible method than the old method of the Holy See, which was limited to a condemnation of Communist doctrine.

Moreover in his lifetime Pius XI made the assertion that he would never shun from holding talks with anybody if they bore the promise of producing some good. In the concern over the fate of mankind and over those values that have been entrusted to the Church the determining factor is not success, which lies only with God, but the effort thereto (see 1 Cor 3:6–8).

Two facts must first of all be made clear. No Pope can acquiesce to the persecution, the oppression of the Church in any country, or allow even that she be subjected to discriminatory difficulties. And no Pope can condone or approve a religious or moral error. Pope John XXIII did neither the former nor the latter. The proclamation of his participation in the fate of the faithful in those countries permeates the whole of his pontificate. In his first radio message to the faithful of the whole world, on October 29, 1958, he found heartfelt words for the expression of this sympathy. Immediately after taking office he sent telegrams expressing his sympathy and solidarity to Cardinals Stepinac and Mindszenty, who had been deprived of their freedom. In the consistory of December 15, 1958 and in the Christmas Message of that same year he again spoke out vigorously on this matter. He announced his intention to convoke a council on the occasion of a prayer hour on behalf of Christians in China on January 25, 1959. He addressed himself to this problem even in his messages to the Christians of individual countries, as in the Brief to the German bishops on December 23, 1958, to the Lithuanian bishops on December 8, 1959, to Archbishop Beran on May 30, 1961, to Cardinal Tien on June 29, 1961, to Hungarian Catholics on December 8, 1962, and to the Slav bishops on May 11, 1963. In 1959 he composed his own prayer for the Silent Church. Even in his other messages, for instance in the homily in St. Paul on April 10, 1960 and in the Easter Message of that year, he expressly made known his sympathy for afflicted Christians. Furthermore in those speeches in which there is no express mention of the oppressed one easily perceives how close they were to his heart—as in the Pentecost homily in 1962.

Truth was a leitmotif in the Pope's thinking, and he never hesitated to say over and over again that the Church must view her loftiest mission to be her self-proclamation. Nevertheless his opening address to the council unmistakeably laid down the form in which John XXIII desired to hear the Church proclaim herself, and he himself also acted accordingly. In short he opted for a positive exposition of the doctrinal and moral truth and against condemnations, from which he did not expect too much, above all when they took place by name and in a form offensive to the parties concerned. He acquiesced to judgments of this kind only when it was unconditionally necessary, as with the decree of the Holy Office dated April 4, 1959, forbidding Catholics to vote for political parties which oppose Christian doctrine. The decree specifically referred to Italy.

Whoever studies the Pope's speeches and messages in a consecutive order will note that from year to year he was increasingly afflicted by a great anxiety: anxiety over world peace. There can certainly be no doubt that this motive was also crucial in relation to the Communist regimes. Pope John repeatedly asserted that peace is one of the highest goods, but also a good that is indivisible. Hence peace must be striven for at all levels of human coexistence and with all available means. He believed it was his duty to fulfill the duty of being *pastor et nauta* in such a way as not to make himself unavailable to anyone, a belief that he solemnly and vigorously reaffirmed in his last great encyclical.

Sources

1. Homily delivered at the Coronation Mass on November 4, 1958, *AAS* 1958, 884–888; convocation of the diocesan synod on January 16, 1960, *AAS* 1960, 179; documents of the synod of January 24–31, 1960, *AAS* 1960, 180–312; promulgation of the decrees on June 29, 1960, *AAS* 1960, 551–544; address of the Pope, *AAS* 1960, 563–567; commission for the revision of the cic, *AAS* 1963, 362–364.

2. Speech upon taking possession of the Lateran, November 23, 1958, AAS 1958, 917. Encyclicals: Ad Petri Cathedram, AAS 1959, 497–531; Sacerdotii nostri primordia, AAS 1959, 545–579; Grata recordatio, AAS 1959, 673–678; Princeps pastorum, AAS 1959, 833–864; Mater et Magistra, AAS 1961, 401–464; Aeterna Dei, AAS 1961, 785–803; Paenitentiam Agere, AAS 1962, 481–491; Pacem in terris, AAS 1963, 257–304.

3. Canonizations: Carolus a Setia and Joachima de Vedruma, AAS 1959, 289–294 and 737–764; Gregorio Barbarigo, AAS 1960, 437–445 and 453–462; Johannes de Ribera, AAS 1960, 129–141 and 497–503; Maria Boscardin, AAS 1961, 289–295 and 705–714; Martin de Porres, AAS 1962, 305–309 and 1963, 193–204; Peter Eymard, Antonio Pucci and Franciscus a Camporubeo, AAS 1963, 5–13; Vincent Pallotti, AAS 1963, 65–74; Laurentius of Brindisi, AAS 1959, 456–461.

Beatifications: Helena Guerra, AAS 1959, 337–342; Maria Dufrost, AAS 1959, 343–348; Innocentius a Bertio, AAS 1961, 803–808; Elizabeth Bayley, AAS 1963, 306–311; Aloysius Palazzolo, AAS 1963, 211–318.

4. Establishment of native hierarchies: Congo, AAS 1960, 372–377; Bahamas, AAS 1961, 249–350; Vietnam, AAS 1961, 84–88 and AAS 1961, 84–88; Indonesia, AAS 1961, 244–248 and 296–299; Korea, AAS 1962, 552–555; Delegations for Scandinavia, AAS 1960, 559–560; Africa, AAS 1960, 1000–1003.

5. Appointments of cardinals: December 1958, AAS 1958, 987–989; December 1959, AAS 1960, 11–12; March 1960, AAS 1960, 326–327; January 1961, AAS 1961, 71; March 1962, AAS 1962, 198–199.

6. Letter to Msgr. Tardini upon his appointment, AAS 1958, 905; to Cardinal Cicognani upon his appointment, AAS 1961, 525–527; vacating of curial offices; participation of all foreign bishops residing in Rome in the plenary sessions of the congregations; appointment of the Patriarchs to the Oriental congregation, AAS 1961, 198, AAS 1962, 253–256; episcopal consecration for all cardinals, AAS 1962, 256–258.

7. Brief to the bishops, April 15, 1962, AAS 1962, 559–565; to Cardinal Urbani, January 3, 1959, AAS 1959, 16–18; to Archbishop Beran, May 30, 1961, AAS 1961, 487–489.

8. Encyclicals: *Sacerdotii nostri primordia*, see 2; address to the Roman clergy, AAS 1960, 967–979; address to the Lateran College, AAS 1958, 1006–1010; address to the College of Propaganda Fide, AAS 1958, 1012–1017; address to the Gregoriana, AAS 1959, 74–79; elevation of the Lateran University, AAS 1959, 401–403; of the Propaganda Fide University, AAS 1962, 755–757; of the Angelicum, AAS 1963, 205–208; Minotum S. Offici on the Biblical Question, AAS 1961, 507; on Teilhard de Chardin, AAS 1962, 526; anniversary speech on the jubilee of the Pontifical Biblical Institute, AAS 1960, 152–158; Apostolic Constitution *Veterum sapientia*, AAS 1962, 129–135.

10. Messages to nations on the occasion of their attainment of sovereignty: Togo, AAS 1962, 403–404; Congo-Leopoldville, AAS 1960, 567–570; Congo-Brazzaville, AAS 1960, 950–951; Upper Volta, AAS 1961, 820–821; Nigeria, AAS 1961, 822–823; state treaty with Austria, AAS 1960, 933–941, 941–945 and 1962, 641–652.

11. Messages to Cardinals Stepinac and Mindszenty, AAS 1958, 904; address in consistory of December 15, 1958, AAS 1958, 983–985; radio message of October 29, 1958, AAS 1958, 838–841; Brief to Cardinal Micara on the prayer hour in St. Paul, AAS 1959, 18–20; Christmas Message 1958, AAS 1959, 11; Brief to the German bishops, AAS 1959, 12–15, to the Lithuanian bishops, AAS 1960, 40–42; to Archbishop Beran, AAS 1961, 487–489; to Cardinal Tien, AAS 1961, 465–469; to Hungarian Catholics, AAS 1963, 534; Prayer for the Silent Church, AAS 1959, 112; homily in St. Paul, AAS 1962, 339–343; Easter Message 1960, AAS 1960, 369–371; Pentecost address 1959, AAS 1959, 419–422; homily on Pentecost 1962, AAS 1962, 437–447; "The Proclamation of the Truth," opening address to the council, AAS 1962, 786–795; decree of the Holy Office on voting during elections, AAS 1959, 271–272; Apostolic Brief *Magnifici eventus* to the Slav bishops.

CARITAS

The Romans spontaneously called John XXIII the "Pope of goodness and the father of the poor." In keeping with his origins and his native disposition John XXIII could not help but be a Pope of Christian *caritas* in a very special way. His testament reads: "Born poor but from honest and humble parents, I am especially glad to die poor. In the service of the Holy Church which has nourished me, I have given away. according to the various requirements and circumstances of my simple and modest life, whatever came into my hands—to a very limited measure for that matter—during the years of my priesthood and episcopacy."

As Apostolic Delegate to Greece and Turkey (1934–1944) Don Roncalli constantly busied himself in both posts with the problems of expellees, of the persecuted and of refugees. Numerous search queries regarding missing persons were processed through him. His delegations, together with the Vatican representations in Berne, Switzerland and in other nonbelligerent countries, were an important link in the worldwide information and search service which his predecessor Pius XII had set up in the Vatican for prisoners of war, missing persons and the members of their families.

Monsignor Roncalli was transferred to Paris (1944–1952)

as Nuncio. Here he administered especially to the needs of German and Italian PWs in France. A good part of his working day was taken up with visits to camps, publishing search notices, passing on news between prisoners and their families, and sending books and other material help to needy persons. He constantly extended help and protection to the unforgotten German pastor in Paris, Abbé Franz Stock (d. 1948). This assistance also took the form of establishing a most unique seminary for PWs in Chartres: PW theology students and priests were withdrawn from other camps in France and brought to Chartres so that they might be able to continue their studies. Nuncio Roncalli had paved the way for the opening of this seminary after negotiations with the French military authorities, also making all the arrangements for the acquisition of the necessary books and supplementary food rations.

A group of priests who had studied in Chartres came to Rome in the summer of 1960. The audience with Pope John turned out to be a cordial "reunion" between the Nuncio and "his" PW seminarians. On this occasion they presented the Pope with a precious chalice as a token of the appreciation of former German PWs in France. In turn he presented it to the German cemetery near St. Peter's in commemoration of the five hundredth anniversary of the religious brotherhood established there.

From the outset Nuncio Roncalli fostered the work of Caritas Internationalis in which Pius XII had wished to see the Church's charitable activity concentrated. At a preparatory session in Paris (1947) the Nuncio addressed the delegates, coming from twenty-seven countries, as the "messengers" of the Holy Father. He fundamentally endorsed the Vatican's wishes as regards charitable activities by referring to the organizaton of the primitive Church and Rome as "the preeminent locus of the community of love" (Ignatius of Antioch).

Already at that time he voiced a fundamental idea which he was later to repeat in audiences, in documents, indeed even during visits to hospitals. It is a major key to an understanding of Pope John: "Seek always that which unites, not that which divides. Give primacy to the positive. We are all children of one Father; as such we wish to come together and to bring the promptings from our spirit and heart before the Holy Father. This obliges him to raise his hand, to give his blessing and to let grow something so great, something which, perhaps, can be viewed as the most manifest miracle of the Church in our time."

Throughout the years of his pontificate, in audiences and in messages, Pope John over and over again referred to the importance of a well ordered charitable activity as an essential feature of Church life. True to the guidelines which he staked out in the great encyclicals *Princeps pastorum* and *Mater et Magistra*, the Pope labored tirelessly to direct the work of Caritas Internationalis increasingly toward assistance to the underdeveloped countries. Under his pontificate the organization encompassed seventy-three national groups. Especially was this the case in connection with those countries which had recently acquired political independence, in which the partnership between state and church is still in the developmental stage in social welfare as well as in other areas. His concern for the welfare of the peoples in the underdeveloped countries made the Pope a frequent speaker before representatives of the FAO, the Food and Agricultural Organization of the United Nations. In special messages Pope John vigorously supported the campaign against hunger in the world, just as he had done in former years when the world was sorely beset by the problem of refugees, through calls to action, financial allotments and special issues of stamps by the Vatican City Post Office.

Since his own means were limited the generous response of the bishops and the faithful to his pleas and directives was a source of great joy and satisfaction to the Pope. As a result there exist today special organizations such as Misereor in Germany, Entraide et Fraternité in Belgium, Fastenactie in Holland and similar groups in France, Switzerland, Austria, the United States, Canada, etc. which conduct carefully planned welfare and assistance programs for the socially and economically underprivileged peoples. At the beginning of the last year of his pontificate Pope John issued a directive urging that this enormous, entirely voluntary "Catholic help for development" be coordinated and organized in such a way as to achieve the highest possible usefulness with the limited means at hand.

At the same time he called for cooperation with other nongovernmental and supra-governmental organizations whenever this was feasible for achievement of the common goal. "We greet the international organizations which in all areas—politics, culture, welfare—wish to serve man in his dignity as a person, as our brother, as a child of God. Catholics are present and active in this honorable competition. And we trust that the number of those who will take this ministry upon themselves with apostolic zeal will grow" (Easter Message, 1963).

Pope John did not restrict his charitable activity to instructions and exhortations to the faithful and to organizations. In times of emergencies and disasters he was always among the first to come to the aid of the afflicted with words of sympathy and with material support.

In 1959 he sent emergency help to twenty-four countries. Among them were the following: Argentina and Brazil (floods), Korea (typhoon), Cuba (victims of the civil war), France (the dam break disaster at Fréjus), Formosa (floods), Japan (tornado), Madagascar (floods). In 1960 seventeen countries were helped by Pope John for similar reasons, among them Chile especially because of the great submarine and land earthquakes. In 1961 the Holy See's assistance program assumed even greater dimensions and extended to many other countries stricken by disaster. Among them were: Burma (floods), Korea and Greece (tornados), Guatemala (volcanic eruption), India and Madagascar (floods). In 1962 help was sent to fifteen countries. Among them were: Columbia (earthquake), Korea (floods), Germany (mine disaster in the Saar belt), Iran (earthquakes and floods), Madagascar and East Pakistan (tornado and floods), Peru (earthquake), Yugoslavia (earthquake).

Many persons individually turned directly to Pope John with their problems. Under his orders the Commissione Soccorsi (Aid Commission) in the Secretariat of State handled more than 56,000 requests for assistance in 1959; 31,000 in 1960; 53,000 in 1961; and 34,227 in 1962.

Letters asking for assistance came from all parts of the
world. For the verification and processing of such requests
the Aid Commission based itself on the Elemosineria
Apostolica for Rome, the Pope's bishopric city, on the POA
(Pontificia Opera Assistenza) for Italy, on Caritas Internationalis and its national organizations, as well as on
papal representations in the different countries. Pope John
personally interested himself in every act of assistance which
in any form could be given to the Church and to the people
behind the Iron Curtain. He viewed even this help as a
means of opening doors and placing the unitive above the
divisive.

Pope John frequently voiced opinions on fundamental
questions in regard to welfare activity. Concerning unity in
the variety of the Christian ministry of charity, he said:

What is especially impressive in the multiple form of your
tasks and in the most different types of institutions is the common disposition which binds and unites everything like the
multi-colored threads of a single, marvelous fabric. Beginning
with the preaching of the truth—to teach the unknowing—up to
the sorrowful assistance to the souls of the departed—to bury
the dead—we traverse in all their variations, the spiritual and
material tribulations of our neighbor who is needy in body or
soul. No one is excluded from this Christian activity of charity.
Those who practice this charitable activity cannot dispense with
the grace which those who devote themselves exclusively to
prayer implore for them. Thus at the deepest level the active
organizations are united with the great contemplative communities of prayer (February 20, 1960).

Discussing the supernatural considerations that must ani-
mate Christian charity, the Pontiff continued:

That which endows your work of love with its true worth however . . . are considerations of a supernatural character. Herein lies the difference between it and all other welfare organizations and activities, for which we have a high esteem and to which we augur success. We are animated by the wish that the spirit of these institutions will also be brought into full harmony with the teaching of the Lord's Prayer. But while practical assistance is the final aim of purely secular institutions it is only a means, a precious one to be sure, but nevertheless always only a means of fulfilling the twofold commandment of love: "Thou shalt love the Lord thy God with thy whole heart, and with thy whole soul, and with thy whole mind . . . Thou shalt love thy neighbor as thyself!" (Mt. 22:37, 39).

In his remarks on charity as an essential activity of the lay apostolate Pope John declared:

We must always keep in view the spiritual beauty of Christian charity in the frame of pastoral care so as not to lose our zeal and the right spiritual disposition. Sometimes we are deeply concerned over the superficiality with which the wrong interpretation of the ten commandments is spread, over the way in which the powerful technical innovations of our time are used, which ought rather to serve your apostolic and civilizing mission. The Church never ceases to raise her voice and to exhort her children to shun this influence. Although our aversion persists, we do not wish to limit ourselves to useless words but to proclaim the works of mercy as a remedy against these abuses. We are certain that evil cannot be checked by means of polemics but only by the means of Christian and benevolent pride with which the treasures of Christianity are shown to the world. . . . It was a great joy for us on December 17, 1959 to listen at the public consistory to the peroration of the canonization process of Frédéric Ozanam. What an example for us still is this apostle of charity! Already in 1833, he and his friends in Paris accomplished great things which were worthy of young Christian students: they prepared themselves for future tasks in society while at the same time devoting themselves to noble and lofty studies.

But the faith with which their hearts was imbued made them perceive that spiritual enrichment must be of service to an intelligent exercise of charity. For only in this way could the world, which had been reawakened by the political and social upheavals of that time, believe in the vitality of Christianity and be conquered by it. For all the great and praiseworthy deeds that are accomplished in the world, caritas that is truly lived and practiced is the only deed that remains and radiates in the purest light unto eternity (February 20, 1960).

Sources

Encyclicals: Mater et Magistra, AAS 1961, 401–464.

Addresses: to the FAO, November 10, 1959, AAS 865–867; on May 3, 1960, AAS 1960, 463–465; on November 22, 1961, AAS 1961, 814.

Radio messages: to the World Nourishment Congress, March 14, 1963, AAS 1963, 344–395; on the occasion of the World Refugee Year, June 28, 1959, AAS 1959, 481–483.

Easter Message 1963. Brief, February 20, 1960, AAS 1960, 147–150.

It is not easy to draw up a balance sheet of the pontificate of John XXIII in relation to the Oriental Church. On the one hand this pontificate staked out very invaluable guidelines as regards the way that can lead to the reestablishment of canonical unity with the Orthodox Church. It established a point of departure for efforts which are now in full swing. On the other hand the Holy See's attitude toward the Orthodox Church has never been wholly free of an element of reservation, indeed of ambivalence, despite all the declarations and all the signs of good will on the part of the Pope himself. Hence at the time of John XXIII's death it seemed difficult to speak of noteworthy successes regarding his policy of rapprochment that he himself had preached and set in motion.

A long stay as Apostolic Delegate in the East (ten years in Bulgaria and ten years in Turkey and Greece) had brought the future John XXIII closer to the problems of the Oriental Church in a way that had never been accessible to any other Pope before him. To be sure, a Leo XIII, a Pius XI were extraordinarily enlightened in this area and they had sponsored many initiatives on the basis of their insight. Nevertheless they started out from considerations

which in the most part were of an abstract character. They
were lacking in that concrete knowledgeableness which experience only can provide.

Monsignor Roncalli was especially suited to acquire precisely this experience thanks to his unusually receptive temperament, the fruit of his great humility. Where others
might be enclosed in the narrow circle of comfortable
prejudices, and might have inattentively walked by, the
future John XXIII showed himself open and ready to view
men and things in a more objective and optimistic light.

His deep understanding of the characteristic traditional
features of the Oriental Church was manifested first and
foremost in his attitude toward the Eastern Church that is
united with Rome. The cordiality with which the Pope
greeted the supreme heads of this Church must have deeply
stirred them because, as will be recalled, they were greatly
aggrieved by certain canonical measures which had been
taken under the previous pontificate. No one was better
equipped than John XXIII to assure them that the Church
of Rome was determined to consider them as fully valid
Catholics, which indeed they are. The high prelates of this
Church were overwhelmed by the cordiality that marked
the audiences, and by the goodness and the understanding
that the Pope showed them. And they were full of hope for
a prompt recognition of their traditional rights, the exercise
of which they demanded for themselves, with all due defer-
ence. All these hopes however have not been immediately
fulfilled. Should we assume that John XXIII reserved a
decision in order to have these rights solemnly confirmed by
the council, an action which in his view would have had

greater weight than a personal decision on his part which could be overruled by one of his successors? This is possible. Actually it would have been wholly in keeping with his style, and humility. But were things really so? This question poses itself upon reading certain passages of the encyclical *Aeterna Dei* (on the occasion of the fifteen hundredth anniversary of the death of Leo the Great). Some very strong turns of phrase in this encyclical engendered pained surprise in many Eastern circles, even among Catholics: theological principles which were expediently referred to at the very moment when the Pope of unity was preparing gestures of such momentous consequence for the reunion of Christians, appeared in the encyclical in amalgamation with historical facts the ambiguity of which still grievously burdens the centuries-old drama of the split between the Eastern and Western factions of Christendom.

The Uniate Eastern Churches also viewed the removal of Cardinal Tisserant from the Sacred Congregation for the Oriental Church with great sorrow and a touch of uneasiness. Doubtlessly John XXIII had plans of his own even here. After a brief interim under Cardinal Cicognani, before he became Secretary of State, the secretarial post of this congregation (of which the Pope himself is prefect) was entrusted to an Eastern prelate, one who had been the assessor of the same congregation. John XXIII did not content himself with this nomination. He also consecrated him a bishop and according to the Byzantine rite during a Mass which the Pope himself celebrated. Such events had never occurred before in the annals of the Popes. Shortly thereafter Bishop A. Coussa was appointed Cardinal. Un-

fortunately Cardinal Coussa died only a few weeks later.
Now Pope John has also departed from this world, and
without revealing the intentions he entertained toward the
Oriental congregation as evidenced by the acceptance of the
Eastern Catholic patriarchs in the Congregation for the Ori-
ental Church in March 1963.

No doubt it is to his sojourn in the East that we must
trace John XXIII's deep and keen feeling regarding the
imperative obligation to work for the reunion of all Christians, especially of those whom he knew best and who are
so close to us through their profession of faith, their loyalty
to the hierarchical, sacramental structure of the Church,
through the treasure of an authentic Eucharist and of all
the sacraments. We would be deluding ourselves were we to
view this tendency merely as a question of sentiment, as a
mere overflow of a deep Christian love. Thenceforth Monsignor Roncalli held very definite views on the problem of
reunion with the Orthodox Church and on the methods
for promoting this unity. In part these views also stemmed
from his friendship with a great pioneer of the idea of
reunion: Canon Lambert Beauduin. In view of the strong
impression which his long contact with this Church had
made on him, and of the deep conviction of her great closeness, it is all the more remarkable that he never, so to speak,
posed the ecumenical problem other than in its full scope
and dimension. We can safely assume that this was not the
result of an inadequate assessment of the deep differences
which distinguish the schism of the Eastern Church from
the split with the confessions that arose out of the Protestant Reformation. Rather with the Pope it was much more

a question, revolving around a justified concern, of not incurring the risk of driving the latter further away, while striving to draw the former closer. In view of the general character of his statements regarding the unity of all Christians, frequently we must actually ponder them in order to grasp that primarily it is the Eastern Churches that are meant. Even in the encyclical *Aeterna Dei* only the historical epoch, discussed in this document, allows the imputation that the encyclical above all concerned these Churches.

Whether this obscureness resulted from a kind of scruple on the part of the Holy Father or from the influence of an adviser, the fact is that he carried this concern so far that certain Orthodox circles, perhaps wholly incorrect, became mistrustful and reproached the Roman Church for professing an ecclesiology which did not take sufficient account of the differences between the Churches and which in addition supposedly avoided coming to terms, ecclesiologically speaking, with her sister Churches in the East. Perhaps this feeling played a role in the decision of the Ecumenical See in Constantinople not to send observers to the council, doing so in the name of all autocephalous Orthodox Churches. We know how the Patriarchate Church in Moscow at the last moment removed herself from this unanimous answer of Orthodoxy, and also how the pastoral greatness common to Pope John XXIII and Patriarch Athenagoras I overcame this temporary untoward incident. We know too that cordial relations between the Roman and Orthodox Churches have been inestimably strengthened by the history-making pilgrimage of Pope John's successor, Paul VI, to the Holy Land, where on two separate occasions

he discussed the problem of unity with Patriarch Athenagoras.

Many may have been astonished over the fact that in this
question Protestant groups showed themselves to be more
receptive than Orthodox groups to the invitation of the
Roman Church. In reality the basic difficulties on the
Orthodox side are less numerous and less serious. On the
other hand the psychological difficulties are all the greater,
to say nothing of the fact that in the last fifty years the so-
called "ecumenical spirit" has undergone an incomparably
lesser development in the East than in the West. In this
sphere John XXIII has shown that he was ahead of his time
vis-a-vis his own curia, as well as in relation to Orthodox
groups. By creating the Secretariat for Promoting Christian
Unity he not only made the Catholic hierarchy, at its highest level, familiar with the problem of unity, he also provided the council with an instrument that is at once suitable
and sufficiently dynamic to carry the cause of unity forward.
The work of the secretariat as regards relations with Prot-
estants has doubtlessly already proved very beneficial; results with respect to the Eastern world have remained
meagre. This is due to the fact that during the preparatory
work in connection with the council the secretariat enjoyed
full freedom in relations with the Protestant world because
no other specialized institute of the curia (apart from the
general authority of the Holy Office) desired to look into
the matter. On the other hand the Roman curia, with
respect to the East, carried on a policy that has been laid
down for centuries, namely that of the Uniate Churches.
It is precisely this policy that runs into passionate opposi-

tion among the Orthodox. As a result of this state of affairs
the responsibility for establishing relations with the Orthodox Churches was entrusted to the Commission for the
Eastern Churches rather than to the secretariat. It was not
long before experience taught that this allocation of responsibility was not a happy one. Moreover it contradicted both
the spirit and letter of the Motu proprio *Superno Dei nutu*
of June 6, 1960. It was not until February 1962 that the
Secretariat for Promoting Christian Unity acquired full
authority in dealing with the separated Eastern Churches.
Only thenceforth could its secretary, Monsignor Wille-
brands, take the first official step to invite observers to the
council. Unfortunately it was not possible to make up for
the lost time. Thus was brought about the well-known
vexatious situation which had not yet been clarified at the
time of the Pope's death. John XXIII however still had
time graciously to accept an official invitation to attend the
Orthodox celebration of the one thousandth anniversary
of the founding of the monastic order on Mount Athos.
The invitation was issued in the name of the organizing
committee of the celebration. Invitations were also sent to
the three great monastic communities of the West: the
Benedictine, the Dominican, the Franciscan. This can be
viewed as a sign of the relaxation of tension on the part of
the Patriarchate of Constantinople, in whose name the invitations were sent. Thus we can look much more hopefully
toward the future with respect to the relations between the
Church of Rome and the separated Eastern Churches.

The release of Monsignor Slipyis, the Metropolitan of
the Uniate Church of Galicia who had been in Soviet im-

prisonment for seventeen years, was one of the greatest
sources of consolation to John XXIII before the all too
early end of his pontificate.

This event was evidence not only of the efforts of the
Holy See on behalf of the fate of one of the Catholic Eastern Churches but also of a change in climate in the relations
with the governments behind the Iron Curtain. Doubtlessly
this belongs to another aspect, to another side of the pontificate of John XXIII. Nevertheless we may not gloss over the
fact that very complicated confessional tangles can possibly
result therefrom.

To sum up: if in its relations with the Christian East
as regards unity the Johannine pontificate could not bring
to fruition everything which the Apostolic Delegate to
Sofia, Istanbul and Athens had hopefully expected, it nevertheless laid down the essential foundations and embarked
upon the first appropriate steps for important later developments.

Will the Secretariat for Promoting Christian Unity solidly establish itself as a permanent body of the Roman
Church as John XXIII had intended from the outset upon
its establishment? It is up to the new Pope to make this
decision. This is a decision which will be all the easier to
make since everything seems to have already been prepared
for the attainment of the goal. In the event of such a development, which we can confidently look forward to, relations
between the Orthodox East and the Secretariat for Promoting Christian Unity will be facilitated further, thanks to the
setting up of a section for this specific purpose within the
frame of this secretariat. It should be noted in this context

that Pope Paul's pilgrimage to the Holy Land from January 4 to 6, 1964, was arranged through a member of this secretariat.

No matter what form the concrete steps of a permanent secretariat may take at the council in the name of the Holy See, what will be even more effective than any step that can be taken concerning the Orthodox Church—as a contribution to the reestablishment of unity with the hitherto separated Oriental Church—is the reestablishment of a deeper theological knowledge and of the institutional structure of the Catholic Church herself through the reappraisal of the collegiate responsibility of the whole episcopate and of the sacramental reality of the Church as a whole. For these are the fundamental ecclesiological facts to which the Christian East, both the Catholic and Orthodox, have justly remained true with a deep inner devotion and conviction. It will be to the imperishable glory of John XXIII that he perceived and laid the foundations for the rapprochement and reunion through the convocation of the council and through the goal and the direction toward which he directed this historic gathering.

Sources

Encyclicals: *Ad Petri cathedram,* AAS 1959, 497–531, *Aeterna Dei,* AAS 1961, 785–803.

Addresses: to the cardinals, January 25, 1959, AAS 1959, 65–69. Following the celebration of the Mass in the Byzantine-Slavonic rite on November 14, 1960 in St. Peter's, AAS 1960, 959–964. At the beginning of the preparations for the council on November 14, 1960, AAS 1960, 1004–1014. On the occasion of the consecration of Cardinal Coussa, AAS 1961, 265–268. To the directors and faithful of the different Oriental rites, AAS 1961, 314–318. To the observer-delegates, AAS 1962, 814–816.

Motu proprio: *Superno Dei nutu*, AAS 1960, 433–437. Brief to Patriarch Maximos IV Saigh in the form of the national language in the liturgy of the Uniate Church, March 31, 1960. Appointment of the Patriarch of the Uniate Eastern Churches as members of the Congregation for the Oriental Church.

WORLD MISSION

As a result of his appointment in 1921 as director of the Society for the Propagation of the Faith in Italy, the future Pope, during the next four years of his life, acquired a comprehensive view of the problem of the work of missions in the modern world and of the curia's mission policy.

Pope John's high esteem of the work of the mission and his conviction of its first-rank importance stem from this period. In the homily delivered at his coronation he described the promotion of the work of the missionary apostolate as the Pope's most important task.

Pope John celebrated his first holy Mass outside the Vatican in the chapel of the College of the Propagation of the Faith. In his first encyclical, *Ad Petri cathedram*, John XXIII confirmed the guidelines of the mission policy of his predecessors (Pius XII, *Evangelii praecones* and *Fidei donum*; Pius XI, *Rerum ecclesiae*).

From the outset, along the lines of Pius XII, he reminded the faithful that the work of the mission is a task that devolves upon the whole Church. Thus he repeatedly urged the episcopate and the faithful to help the Churches in mission countries materially and spiritually. Further he exhorted the latter to use this help which they received with

an eye on the welfare of the whole Church. In keeping
with the progressive emancipation of the Afro-Asiatic countries and the "nationalistic wave" bound up with this development, and in order to counter the possibility that
Communism might endanger or inundate the liberation
movements in these continents, John XXIII accelerated the
establishment of native hierarchies—which had been already
started by Pius XII—especially in Africa, and the internationalization of the College of Cardinals. On March 28,
1960, for the first time in history, a native of Central Africa,
Monsignor Tatsuo Doi, received the cardinal's hat.

Pope John's encyclical on missions, *Princeps pastorum*,
is almost exclusively devoted to the problems of firmly
rooting and consolidating the Church in the countries that
had recently acquired their independence. In view of the
"growing rich harvests" which were "endangered by the
enemies of God," it dealt with the formation of a native
clergy and the tasks incumbent upon the laity in the work
of missions. The salient passages of the encyclical stress the
following:

Native candidates for the priesthood, when possible,
should be instructed and trained by native priests. They
must receive a "complete" priestly education but they must
"not be unduly separated from their social world." They
must "enjoy the permissible freedom of thought and action," and indigenous and foreign missionaries are to enjoy
"full equality."

Instruction and education in the Christian faith must
not be limited to the teaching of the catechism and to
making known the most important moral commandments

in a summary form because this would mean "to lead an inert people to the Church." Preparation for the apostolate must take place in a special way with all peoples "who have special indigenous rites of initiation." The form of the apostolate must be adapted to local conditions and requirements "because it is simply impossible to apply what has successfully prevailed in one place indiscriminately elsewhere." Due to the difficulty of leaving the formation of the leading forces of Catholic Action exclusively to school instruction, the local ordinaries "should open schools for the apostolate, in a regular way and in the best possible form, whose educational program naturally is distinguished from that of the regular school." A special importance is attached to the activity of Christian lay persons in mission countries. The cooperation between priests and lay persons must aim at a division of labor.

Thus social enterprises and agencies involving aid to underdeveloped countries "should be entrusted as soon as possible to native men and women, so that missionaries may devote all their energies to the preaching of the gospel. . . ." Finally the encyclical stresses the special importance of making contact with educated persons and intellectuals, the necessity of establishing centers for studies and teaching, and for spreading and increasing Catholic literature. But the encyclical also expresses an awareness of inherent limitations: "Not everywhere can everything be done."

Pope John's emphasis on strengthening the roots of the mission Churches and on the personal responsibility of Asian and African lay persons was not limited to the ecclesiastical sphere. The responsibility of the laity was to keep step with the requirements of the historical moment even where it might include tasks which could be carried out only by the universal Church as a whole, according to his oft-repeated and proclaimed conviction. The Pope also emphasized the connection and the dependent relation between the social order and the development of a spiritual-moral life. Consequently his admonitions to the faithful frequently were followed by appeals to statesmen to create the social and political pre-conditions thereto and not to destroy the seed of the proclamation of the gospel.

This applies in a special way to his Briefs and messages to Latin American countries. They remained among the Pope's major concerns until the end. As late as May 31, 1963 he had a talk with the Cardinal Secretary of State in which he laid down directives as to how existing Latin American institutions might intensify their pastoral activity. Despite the little time that was left him, Pope John's efforts with regard to this continent have borne visible fruit: exchanges of priests, adaptation of the Hispanic legacy to present-day requirements, the activization of the religious orders. As regards the mission fields in Asia and Africa, we cannot for the time being foresee what the results of the council will be, namely those that will ensue from the contacts made and the undertakings that were planned at this historical gathering.

On Pentecost 1960 Pope John XXIII sent three additional native bishops to the Chinese Church in exile, as a sign of promise to the persecuted Church of China that she would live again.

Sources

Encyclical on missions: *Princeps pastorum*, AAS 1959, 853–864.

Encyclicals with strong references to missions: *Ad Petri cathedram*, AAS 1959, 497–531; *Sacerdotii nostri primordia*, AAS 1959, 545–579; *Mater et Magistra*, AAS 1961, 401–464; *Pacem in terris*, AAS 1963, 257–304.

Apostolic Briefs: *Quotiescumque* to Cardinal Tien Shen-sin, AAS 1961, 465–469; *Quod dilectum* to the bishops of India, August 20, 1960, AAS 1960, 805–808; *Iam in Pontificatus* to the bishops of Vietnam, January 14, 1961, AAS 1961, 84–88.

Briefs: *Ad dilectos* to the bishops of Latin America, AAS 1962, 28–31; *Si ingratae* to the bishops of Argentina, May 11, 1959, AAS 1959, 417–419; to the German bishops on priestly help for Latin America, January 11, 1961.

Important addresses: to the Third Congress of the Latin American Bishops' Conference; to the secret consistory (on the Chinese schism), January 15, 1958, AAS 1958, 981–986; to young missionaries, October 11, 1959, AAS 1959, 766–769; to the consistory, March 28, 1960, AAS 1960, 321–326; to the heads of the religious orders in Latin America, March 25, 1960, AAS 1960, 344–349; to the newly consecrated mission-bishops, May 8, 1960, AAS 1960, 466–469, and May 21, 1961, AAS 1961, 358–362; to the Catholics of Africa, June 5, 1960, AAS 1960, 474–477; to the consistory, January 16, 1961, AAS 1961, 66–70.

Decrees and regulations of the congregations: Apostolic Lay Activity in Latin America (Cardinal Mimmi to Cardinal Cushing); decree of the Consistorial Congregation concerning liturgical privileges in Latin America and in The Philippines, August 8, 1959, AAS 1959, 915–918.

CHRISTIAN UNITY

1. From the very first day of his pontificate the invitation to separated Christians to return to the bosom of the Church was one of Pope John's dominant leitmotifs. He understood this call to unity in terms of his duty as the good shepherd and brother to all, indeed even in terms of strict dogma: no one arrives at the sheepfold of Jesus Christ save under the guidance of the Pope; there is no salvation without fellowship with him. In his first radio message Pope John expressly invited "the whole Church of the East to return, immediately and voluntarily, to the common parental household." This invitation was extended in a spirit of pronounced gentleness and humility. The first Christmas Message repeated the call, again with an eye directed more toward the Orthodox Churches. The public announcement of the ecumenical council, made on January 25, 1959, spoke of the "invitation to the separated communities to seek unity." Later the official promulgation mentioned the "renewed invitation to the faithful of the separated communities so that they too may follow us in a friendly way in this quest for unity and grace." The Eastern Churches also occupied the foreground in his subsequent addresses. Utterances such as: "We do not wish to hold an historical trial, our aim is not to point out who was right and who was wrong. The responsibility is shared on both sides. We want merely to say: let us come together, let us put an end to the divisions," apply specifically to the Eastern Churches.

Any misunderstandings prevailing in the *oekumenia* concerning the catholicity of the council were cleared up by the pronouncement that the council should be "an invitation to the separated brethren, who glory in the name of Christians, so that they may return to the universal flock, the guidance and protection of which Christ entrusted to St. Peter in an unshakeable commandment of his divine will." The council was to extend this invocation as a sign of holy harmony. The stages along the way to reunion with the Eastern Church were more closely marked out (first rapprochement, then cooperation). Section III in *Ad Petri cathedram*, entitled "Church Unity," cautiously appealed to the ecumenical movement as well as to the "movement of sympathy for the faith and institutions of the Catholic Church and a constantly growing esteem for the Apostolic See." This was combined with a rigid exposition of the traditional Roman concepts of unity.

2. Pope John's first universal prayer intention for January 1960 reflected his abiding pastoral concern: "May all those who are seeking for the true Church more deeply perceive the desire of the heart of Jesus for the unity of his children and thereby be led to unity." Cardinal Secretary of State Tardini discussed the main line of ecumenical procedure at a press conference held on October 30, 1959: there was no probability of an invitation to the representatives of the

separated Churches but those representatives who wished
to do so could certainly be present as observers. At any rate
the most important preparatory documents would be
brought to their attention so that they could adopt a private
position in regard to them. Ecumenical cooperation was to
be carried out by the Secretariat for Promoting Christian
Unity, established on Pentecost 1960, at the same time as
the conciliar commissions "in order that our love and our
good will toward Christians separated from the Apostolic
See may stand out even more visibly, and in order that the
latter can more easily follow the work of the council and
find the way to achieve that unity which Jesus beseeched
from his heavenly Father." The first act of the Secretariat,
under the direction of Cardinal Bea, was the private reception that the Pope tendered the Primate of the Church
of England, Archbishop Geoffrey Fisher of Canterbury, on
December 2, 1960. This led to the appointment of a permanent representative of the Archbishop of Canterbury to
the Secretariat for Promoting Christian Unity and it also
ushered in visits from many other ecumenical church leaders, all of whom came on their own initiative. The most
important of these visits were the following: on November
15, 1961 Bishop Arthur Lichtenberger, Protestant Episcopal Church, U.S.A.; on December 20, 1961 D. Jackson,
President of the National Baptist Convention, U.S.A.; on
October 15, 1962 Fred P. Corson, President of the World
Conference of Methodists; on February 8, 1963 Leslie
Davidson, President of the Conference of Methodists of
Great Britain; on February 25, 1963 Roger Schutz, the Prior

of Taizé; and on March 28, 1963 Archibald C. Craig, Moderator of the Presbyterian Church of Scotland.

Shortly before, Pope John had presented a pastoral council program to the members of the commissions in which the intriguing formula of the opening address of October 11, 1962 was repeated: in contrast to former councils this time it was more than a question of this or that point of doctrine or discipline which had to be called back to the pure sources of revelation and tradition; rather it was a question of "the substance of human and Christian thought and life," the "pivot to which every baptized person must hold fast." Membership in the Church is not merely a simple mark of an individual character in each person. Rather it is of an eminently social character. The teaching regarding the Church as preached by the apostle Paul in 1 Corrinthians, verse 12, is another illustration of the Church's evangelical idea. It was quoted as evidence of Catholic unity from which countless groups are separated and to which, nevertheless, they are desirous of returning.

3. Meanwhile Cardinal Bea elaborated the guidelines of Pope John's pastoral method in order to create an atmosphere of "fellowship in Christ" by recognizing the baptism of all Christians and by treating them as "brothers in Christ." As a result the different communities acquired confidence in the Pope and were ready to send observers to the council. There was no talk of possible doctrinal discussions on the subject of reunion but there certainly was talk of a greater clarification in regard to dogmas. Nevertheless the encyclical *Aeterna Dei* on Pope Leo I formulated the concept of Church unity with the same strictness as *Ad Petri*

cathedram. It called for a return to and a union with the
Bishop of Rome in the spirit of Chalcedon, doing so at a
time just after the Orthodox had entered the World Council of Churches in New Delhi and had ignored the "unity"
document, which contained no clarifications of a dogmatic
nature. The Apostolic Constitution *Humanae salutis* was
promulgated December 25, 1961. It dealt with the convocation of the Second Vatican Council and declared that the
fundamental truths of the faith ought to receive a greater
elucidation and that the preconditions of reciprocal love be
created "so that the desire for unity among the Christians
separated from the Apostolic See may be quickened further
and thus smooth the road back for them."

At the height of Pope John's pontificate prominence was
given to the point of view which held that the way to the
reunion of separated Christians could also be smoothed by
a return of the Church to the purity of her origins. Further
Catholics were urged to strive for a greater appraisal and a
more exact knowledge of separated Christians (General
Prayer Intention for May 1962). There was also a strengthening of the theme acknowledging that formulations of
dogma contained presuppositions that were conditioned "by
considerations of an ideological-historical character" (Cardinal Bea on May 22, 1962 in Munich). Moreover, during
the selection of the Christian communities that were to be
invited, all ecclesiological requirements were dropped. The
only requirements laid down were that the communities
have "a certain constancy" and show a real interest in the
invitation and a readiness to maintain friendly contact.
Only non-Christian religions were excluded from considera-

tion. Just before the beginning of the council Cardinal Bea went to Moscow for negotiations with the Russian Orthodox Church. He succeeded in winning this Church over to the idea of sending observers because Pope John had combined his deeply felt ecumenical concerns with a plan for peace.

Pope John found a provisional method of ecumenical cooperation for making Christian unity manifest by the inclusion of observers in the conciliar proceedings. This plan met with everybody's satisfaction. They were filled with hope by the declaration in the opening address wherein Pope John made a distinction between the substance of doctrine and its historically conditioned formulation, as well as by his conception of a threefold plan of unity of the Church with all Christians and men of good will. Pope John gave convincing expression to this vision with his fatherly words at the "familial and intimate" reception tendered the observers at the ecumenical council on October 13, 1962. Later he was to confirm this vision with the vow that he took on his deathbed: "I burn to work and to suffer for the approach of that hour in which the prayer of Jesus at the Last Supper will be a reality for all."

Other documents added nothing essentially new. Talk of a "return" of the separated brethren was even dropped. On November 20, 1962 Pope John dramatically intervened in the conciliar vote on the revelation schema, which had bogged down. His stand in favor of its revision in the ecumenical spirit, as espoused by Cardinal Bea and as desired by the majority of the council Fathers, was one of the most convincing demonstrations of the ecumenical sincerity of his pontificate.

Sources

Encyclicals: *Ad Petri cathedram*, AAS 1959, 497–531; *Aeterna Dei*, AAS 1961, 785–805.

Motu proprio: *Superno Dei nutu*, AAS 1960, 433–437; Apostolic Constitution *Humanae salutis*, AAS 1962, 5–13.

Addresses: radio message, October 29, 1958, AAS 1958, 838–841; Coronation homily, AAS 1958, 884–888; Christmas Message 1958, AAS 1959, 5–12; Address in St. Paul with the announcement of the council, AAS 1959, 65–69; address to the representatives of Catholic universities, AAS 1959, 299–301; *Adhortatio* to the Venetian clergy, AAS 1959, 375–381; Address to the council commissions, AAS 1960, 1004–1014; address to the observer-delegations at the council, AAS 1962, 814–816.

Coexistence in Justice and Peace

1. Social themes occupied a prominent place in the doctrinal and pastoral pronouncements of Pope John XXIII. The two most comprehensive as well as the two most important encyclicals of his pontificate were dedicated to themes of a social character. The first encyclical, *Ad Petri cathedram*, and many later occasional addresses, already gave evidence of the Pope's efforts to show the way to the Church and to men of good will through the tangle of the immense social transformations and dislocations of our era. At the express wish of the Pope the efforts to engender a social orientation among Catholics that would be in keeping with the Christian message of the Church, and to elucidate the social mission of the Church—especially of the laity—were accepted in the agenda of the conciliar preparatory work and discussions.

One fact is of crucial importance in Pope John's exposition of Catholic social doctrine: despite the closest bond existing between him and the tradition of his predecessors, John XXIII realized that "the situation already changed during the period mentioned by Pius XII has undergone in these two decades profound transformations." Consequently he strove to deal with new themes: structural re-

form of agriculture, economic and social balance between
the industrially advanced and the underdeveloped countries,
international disarmament and armament control. Another
theme was expressed in the demand for the establishment
of a worldwide organization for the promotion of universal
welfare. This would be in keeping with the original unity of
mankind and the rapid joint growth of countries and continents in the modern world. Pope John also discussed in
great detail other themes which had been merely touched
upon by his predecessors. Above all he was able to strike
new notes in Catholic social teaching in more than one
problem area.

Many of these new notes were sounded in *Mater et Magistra*. They were sounded even more distinctly in *Pacem in
terris* in connection with the special subject matter of the
encyclical. Here we shall refer to some of these new emphases which not only involve central formulations of Catholic
social teaching but also touch upon a very sensitive nerve-
development of the present-day economic and social structure.

In the socio-political sphere these new emphases constitute a qualified and more comprehensive understanding of
modern industrial society organized on the basis of large-
scale production. A clearer position, adapted to present-day
development, is taken on a system of economic enterprise
still awaiting an ethical and dispassionate justification.
There is also a recognition of the "very difficult problem" of
property, which is viewed more in functional-dynamic than
in legal-static terms. On a socio-political level they constitute a careful weighing of the positive and negative factors

"of the growing number of social interlacings," a qualified view of the state and its obligations in connection with the achievement and maintenance of the common good, as well as of supra-governmental organizations. Correspondingly a more positive attitude is taken toward intermediate bodies, associations and organizations of a social character, especially trade unions, and their contribution to making peaceful cooperation on a national and international scale a reality.

2. His predecessor, Pius XII, had already dealt with the problems of agriculture. He showed an awareness of the signs of decline in this sector of the economy, and pondered its capacity to compete vis-a-vis with other branches of production. But *Mater et Magistra* was the first papal document to provide a total exposition of the problem, combined with comprehensive and concrete proposals for reform. No longer is the exodus from the land viewed as a striving for greater material gain and as an escape from the restrictions and responsibility of one's social status. Rather it is appraised as a mass phenomenon which, despite other "multiple factors," is connected with the development of society as a whole. In his encyclical Pope John observes that the farming sector "almost everywhere is a depressed area." The corrective measures proposed are not limited to a mere appeal to check the flow of population from rural areas. Rather they call for a "structural agrarian policy" based on family-sized farms as a "community of persons;" these farms are "ideally suited for this sector of production." Farmers, cooperatives for the promotion of agriculture, and the state must equally cooperate in its "ultimate" realization. The

state should establish a credit and fiscal policy in keeping with these efforts and structure the market, fixing the prices of agricultural products "so that they are within the means of all consumers."

Like his predecessor, Pope John also called for the creation of infra-structures and for the technical improvement of production through matching investments and the technical training of farmers. On the assumption that the exodus from the land could not be checked for the time being, the Pope also urged that those leaving the land be given "every kind of assistance" which they might need "in order to integrate themselves in the new environment."

3. In Pope John's view the problem of economic balance between underdeveloped countries and modern industrial nations constitutes "one of the great tasks facing our time." This problem had already been touched upon marginally by Pius XI, and Pius XII had dealt with it in a more fundamental way only in the last years of his pontificate.

Although he took cognizance of the attempts already undertaken for the solution of the problem, Pope John called for a worldwide "active solidarity" to which individuals, social associations and organizations and governments were equally summoned. The Church is duty bound to be of every possible assistance. The solidarity to which the pope summoned the world is to be carried out in practical measures of assistance whereby "the errors of the past" are to be avoided and the "economic and social rise" of peoples is to be reciprocally balanced without incurring the risk of "a new colonialism" or doing social or cultural violence to these peoples "with their wholly definite features that characterize them." Rather the advanced countries should also transmit spiritual values along with their material assistance to the underdeveloped lands. The Church especially must prove herself "as the Church of the poor." Pope John was optimistic in his utterances on the contrast between over-population and the means of sustenance. "Considered on a world scale, the relationship between the population increase on the one hand, and the availability of food supplies on the other, does not seem—at least for the moment and in the near future—to create a difficulty." The solution of the problems bound up with this disparity is a matter of scientific and technical organization, and of just distribution. They must also be viewed in a moral framework.

4. Pope John also went very far in his call for a coordinating public authority, one having worldwide power, that would effectively work for the realization of the universal common good. The Pope of course considered regional and political organizations but he concentrated most strongly on international questions. In his view a world public authority is not only feasible in principle but imperative for the sake of the common good. For the very reason that economics, culture and progress are internationally intertwined, "the leaders of individual nations cannot solve this problem in a satisfactory way." Neither regional public authorities nor treaties between states suffice for "safeguarding security and peace in the whole world." Nevertheless Pope John was not projecting the idea of world government. The principle of subsidiarity, which leaves individual rights to individual nations, must be observed upon the realization of an international community of nations, despite the consequent

limitation of the principle of sovereignty and of the formation of regional blocs. Furthermore a "political power . . . whose authority should be recognized all over the world" must not be set up by force against the will of individual countries. Pope John did not underestimate the enormous difficulties in the way of establishing such an institution. In his opinion the United Nations, whose universal Declaration of the Rights of Man contains an ethical basis acceptable to all—despite some revisions that are justifiably called for—constitutes a possible, available point of departure in the direction of the juridico-political organization of the world community.

5. Certain shifts in emphasis that have become manifest within the traditional doctrinal heritage of the Church are of no less importance for the further development of Catholic social teaching, especially along the lines of a concrete and progressive adjustment to the given structure of modern economic society. This applies first of all to the phenomenon of socialization, the essential features of which were already described in the message which the Cardinal Secretary of State sent to the 47th annual "Social Week" in France. They were further elaborated in *Mater et Magistra.* Pope John attempted to deal with this phenomenon in all its aspects. He did not gloss over the hazards it entails: the interference of society and the state in areas "which belong to man's most personal aspects," the narrowing of the individual's sphere of freedom, the growing dependency of the individual on society. But Pope John also minimized these hazards because the progressive multiplication of relations are to be viewed as "the fruit and expression of a natural

Sotto il Monte with its medieval tower.

The house in which Angelo Giuseppe Roncalli was born.

Pope John's parents and his three brothers.

Angelo Roncalli as a theology student, as a sergeant in the medical corps, and as bishop.

Archbishop Roncalli (upper extreme right) as Nuncio in Istanbul, and as Nuncio in France (below) consecrating priests in the Chartres prisoner-of-war seminary for German theology students.

Archbishop Roncalli as Nuncio in Paris in the studio of the sculptor Bartellety, who fashioned a bust of the future Pope, and (below) in conversation with Édouard Herriot, President of the National Assembly, and Jean Baylot, the Prefect of Police.

Archbishop Roncalli as the Nuncio in Paris in conversation with Robert Schumann (above), and at the moment of receiving his cardinal's hat from the President of the French Republic, Vincent Auriol.

As Patriarch of Venice during an *Ad-Limina* visit with Pius XII, and as Patriarch of Venice with Cardinal Ottaviani in front of St. Mark's Cathedral. Picture below shows Patriarch Roncalli with Cardinal Wyszynski.

John XXIII, just before imparting the blessing *Urbi et Orbi* at his coronation.

Pope John XXIII during the ceremony of the washing of feet in the Lateran Basilica

and during his second visit to the Regina Coeli prison in Rome.

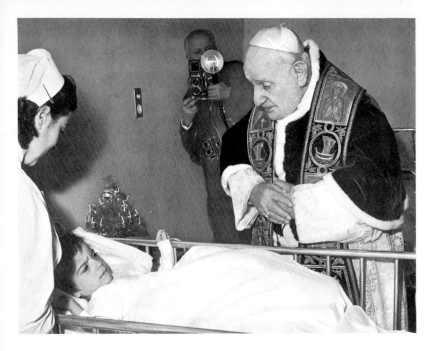

John XXIII during his visit to the children's hospital "Bambino Jesu," and to a home for retired priests.

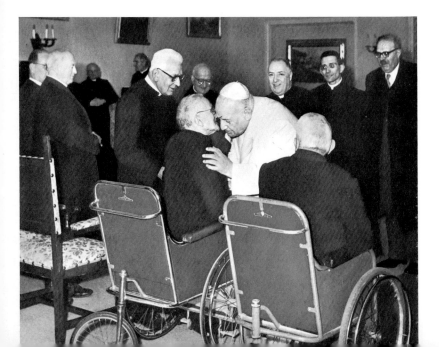

The Pope receives the Prime Minister of Burma, U Nu (upper left), a high Shinto priest from Japan (upper right), a high Lama from Tibet (bottom left), and an Indian boy from the Navajo tribe.

Pope John with
President Eisen-
hower (above), and
Queen Elizabeth
and Prince Philip.

Pope John receives Chancellor Konrad Adenauer of the German Federal Republic (above), and Jacqueline Kennedy, wife of the late American President.

John XXIII with the first Negro Cardinal, Laurian Rugambwa, and with Ukrainian Archbishop Josef Slipyi, Metropolitan of Lemberg, after his liberation from eighteen years of enforced labor in Siberia.

A view of the opening day ceremony of the Second Vatican Council in St. Peter's Basilica.

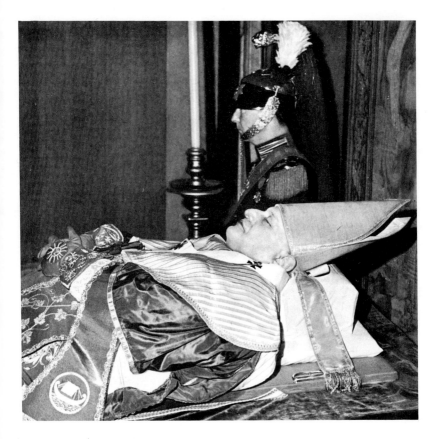

John XXIII lying in state at the Vatican.

tendency, almost irrepressible, in human beings." Socialization is not to be considered "a product of natural forces working in a deterministic way, but a creation of men, conscious beings, free and intended by nature to work in a responsible way." Socialization can be realized in a manner so "as to draw from it the advantages contained therein and to remove or restrain the negative aspects."

For this three prerequisites are necessary: a healthy social ethos among individuals, among groups and among public (governmental) authorities, an effective autonomy on the part of intermediate bodies in keeping with the subsidiary structure of society, and finally the creation of primary social bodies as communities of persons. Further this process is not to be viewed and actualized under its purely economic aspects. Social progress and social development should go hand in hand. The Pope considered this double requirement to be of crucial importance.

6. Pope John desired to see relations between capital and labor geared to the demands for a balanced adjustment between economic and social progress. Despite the observation that "in many lands and entire continents countless workers are being paid wages which condemn them and their families to subhuman conditions of life," the Pontiff hailed the relaxation of tensions between capital and labor and between the various strata of society as one of the most felicitous signs of our era. In the large-scale industrial organizations of modern economic society, Pope John saw a normal structural element of industrial society that must absolutely be combined with the common good. He was the first Pope in history to give a comprehensive structural anal-

ysis of large-scale industry. He proposed that the highest
maxim which should guide the equitable restructuring of
the economic system should be that of transforming economic enterprises into genuine communities of persons.
Thus not only the distribution of social products but also
the sum total of achievements in the economic sphere
would be in keeping with the requirements of justice.

Following a line of thought expounded by Pius XII, Pope
John emphatically called for the active participation of
workers "in the activity of the enterprises to which they
belong." At the same time he recognized that the concrete
form of participation could not be defined once and for all
because its specific conditions are subject "to quick and substantial change in the very same enterprise." *Mater et Magistra* obviously deliberately avoided the term "co-manage-
ment" which is bound up with so many other questions.
The question regarding the extent to which participation is
to concern social matters and such which directly or indirectly concern the direction of enterprises (economic co-
management) was formally left open. Despite the emphasis
placed on "the efficiency of the unity of direction" it can be
inferred from the context that the possibility of definite
forms of economic participation such as co-ownership—
whereby the concrete form of its realization again is left
open—is again viewed as possible and even required under
certain circumstances because "the exercise of responsibility
on the part of the workers in enterprises corresponds to the
lawful demands inherent in human nature." Active worker
participation should not be limited to the individual pro-
ductive unit. Workers should bring their views and weight

to bear "in all areas of social life." A prominent and express role is assigned to trade unions as the legitimate representatives of the workers at all levels. Christian trade unions in particular are encouraged to undertake even greater efforts in their promotion of working class interests. Also singled out for praise are those Catholics "imbued with Christian principles who perform excellent work in other professional groups and trade unions, taking their aspiration from the natural principles of dealing with each other and respecting the freedom of conscience."

7. In his discussions on the relation between private initiative and government intervention Pope John followed the pronouncements of his predecessors. Further limits were set to the inroads of governmental authority, although at the same time the broadest possibilities in this direction were expressly recognized. Governmental authority ought to be active in an economic-political sense "in multiple ways," more comprehensively and systematically than formerly "and [should] establish suitable institutions and modalities for this purpose." But the ultimate goal of governmental interventions should be the broadening of true private initiative and not its abolition. Pope John championed the fundamental right to private property, "even in the means of production," with the same resoluteness he exhibited in his espousal of private initiative as a dynamo of economic and social life. Indeed it was with a certain approval that he cited "political associations and organizations that formerly denied the natural right to property" but that today "taught by social development altogether recognize this right."

Property however is indissolubly linked to social obligation, an obligation deriving from "property itself." It re-
quires a broader distribution of property and the creation of
property-relations that are geared to the needs of workers
because "property lives on the fruitfulness of labor and
receives its importance from it."

Pope John did not take a dim view of the fact that today
many place greater confidence in a skilled occupation or in
income deriving from work or rights based on work rather
than in income deriving from property, despite the exten-
sive changes in the forms and relations of property ensuing
therefrom. No objections can be raised against the broadening of public property within the framework of the common
good because the state "for the sake of the common good"
must undertake even greater tasks.

8. Pope John's whole social teaching is based on the principles of personality, of subsidiarity, of solidarity and of the
common good. The outline of a possible social order rooted
in peace was sketched more clearly in *Pacem in terris* than in
Mater et Magistra. The order of the universe established by
God rests upon the aforementioned four principles. Everything of a social character has its origin in the personality of
man and must be understood according to the laws of his
nature and not according to those of "the irrational forces
and elements of the universe." Consequently everything
bearing a social character relates to the person and must
serve to effect personal fulfillment. The essential subsidiarity
position of all social institutions and structures rests on this
basis. The ethical categories of right and of duty are to be
applied to all social structures, groups, organizations, nations

and communities of nations, just as they are applied to individuals. Only with a full knowledge and actualization of the rights and duties of the individual and of the different social groups can a universal order of peace be attained in which the common good—which is the *raison d'être* of all authority—will be guaranteed for all.

Pope John interpreted the "signs of the times," as they appear in the personal, social and individual sphere, in the light of the social imperatives deriving from basic rights, the catalogue of which he broadened. Peace can be realized only on the basis of a social order in which the rights and the duties of the individual, of social groups and associations and of nations are respected. Therefore three essential aspects, i.e. the personal, the social and the international, are to be examined in the structuring of such an order of peace. Peace cannot be the result of a balance of power between political and military powers. Ultimately it is an expression of an attitude of peace which thrives on the ethos of the individuals and on societal energies.

9. In the face of the threats of war Pope John missed no opportunity to admonish all responsible governmental leaders to maintain and safeguard peace. In many addresses he pointed out how international peace depended on the "peace of the heart" and on social peace. His practical efforts on behalf of peace were guided by three considerations, all of which were essentially determined by the Pope's conception of his ecclesiastical office:

a) From the beginning of his pontificate he considered himself, because of his office, as standing above contending political parties and blocs. He hoped that all would heed the

Pope whose action "is not influenced by any earthly aim and any claim to political power."

b) Pope John was of the opinion that the tasks facing both the social apostolate of the Church and her mission of peace would be facilitated by a clear distinction and an unmistakeable *de facto* separation between the exercise of political power and the routine administration of ecclesiastical office as such. This was why he strove to release the Church from every kind of political hold and to recall the "essential and complete neutrality of the Church." Pope John put this separation into practice despite opposition within Italy and from the Italian political parties. On this point he knew that he was in fundamental agreement with responsible Catholic lay persons.

c) Pope John was deeply disposed to see the possibility of good, or at least its beginning, in the energies shaping present-day society. Nevertheless he never failed to censure ideologies and systems hostile to the Church. Precisely for this reason it must be borne in mind that "false philosophical teachings regarding the nature, origin and destiny of the universe and of man cannot be identified with definite historical movements concerned with economic, social, cultural or political questions, not even when these movements have originated from those teachings and still draw inspiration from them."

10. The complete exposition of Catholic social doctrine culminated in the call that it be transformed into reality. Catholics should not only "frequently consider" the "social principles and directives that have been learned" but also translate them into deeds. The positive worldwide response

to *Mater et Magistra* was followed by an urgent papal exhortation for the actualization of the teachings expounded in that encyclical. He called especially for measures of a socio-pedagogical character and demanded that the social doctrine of the Church be included in the curricula of Catholic schools and training programs "as an integrating component of the Christian conception of man." A role of first-rank importance was assigned to the laity in translating the social teaching of the Church into reality. The laity's practical activity is to be guided by the following concrete principles:

a) Christians must become aware of the social reality in which they live and not withdraw into a false inwardness.

b) The presence of the law "of success" for Catholics too when it is a question of bringing "the principles of authentic humanity in harmony with the teaching of the Gospel." It is expedient to make use of all available technical and personal means, including modern mass media, for the propagation and the realization of the Church's social doctrine.

c) The lay person's personal responsibility, as this is established by existing, de facto social and political regulations, is to be preserved. Obviously the latter may not be contrary to the Church's teachings. Nevertheless a healthy pluralism of views is to be welcomed in this area.

d) The social action of Catholics is essentially to be viewed as a service to the community and must not be limited to one's own group. Catholics should "test other views with the benevolence due them"—without of course compromising on matters of faith and morals. Furthermore Catholics should not "merely focus on their own interests" but also be mindful of their duty to cooperate loyally and disinterestedly with others.

The objection has been raised that Pope John's exposition of Catholic social doctrine is untheological. This objection is correct in a formal sense if thereby one means to say that the analysis of principles is given lesser prominence in order to endow the social imperative with a more concrete character. As a matter of fact Pope John's social teaching is geared more to the actualities of present-day social development than it is to definite schools of thought on social morality. It is indisputable that the Pope's social doctrines, including the conclusions that are ultimately drawn therefrom, are based on the message of the bible and on natural law as the Church understands it. That Pope John renounced a systematic discussion of principle in favor of what can be concretely achieved and that he strove to derive practical imperatives from the principle of personal fulfillment actually validates the Church's social doctrine and the practical activity based upon it. We can correctly understand his social teachings if we see the mission of the Church in the world as Pope John envisaged it. According to him it is indisputable that the Church must ceaselessly point out to man his ultra-mundane destiny. But precisely for this reason the Church must "also concern herself with everyday needs" in accordance with the example of the Lord, who commiserated with the hungry and the needy. By following this example Pope John, even in his social pronouncements, was not only to reiterate incontestable principles and to condemn errors, but also to apply the "remedy of compassion."

Sources

Encyclicals: *Mater et Magistra*, AAS 1961, 401–464; *Pacem in terris*, AAS 1963, 257–304.

1. Encyclical *Ad Petri cathedram*, AAS 1959, 497–531; homily on the first anniversary of his coronation, November 4, 1959, AAS 1959, 814–818; Christmas Message 1960, AAS 1961, 5–15; address on peace, September 10, 1961, AAS 1961; radio message, September 11, 1962, AAS 1962, 678–685; Easter Message 1963; Address of May 15, 1961.

6. Encyclical *Ad Petri cathedram*, AAS 1959, 497–531.

8. Address to the representatives of governments at the opening of the council, October 12, 1962, AAS 1962, 814–819; Christmas Message 1960, AAS 1961, 5–15.

9. Address on peace, September 10, 1961, AAS 1961, 577–582; radio message, October 25, 1962, AAS 1962, 861–862; Christmas Message 1959, AAS 1960, 27–35; Encyclical *Ad Petri cathedram*, AAS 1959, 497–531.

LETTER TO HIS BROTHER ZAVERIO

The Vatican
December 3, 1961

My dear brother Severo,

Today is the feast of your great patron—the one of your real and actual name—St. Francis Xavier, as our dear *barba* was called and now happily our nephew Zaverio.*

I believe three years have gone by since I stopped using a typewriter, which I used to like to do so much. If today I have decided to resume the habit and to use a machine which is brand new and all mine, I have done so in order to tell you that I know that I am growing old despite all the fuss that was made over my birthday. Nevertheless I continue to feel well and I am on the way back to good health, even if some minor disturbances remind me that I am 80 and not 60 or 50 years old. For the moment, at least, I can carry on the good service of the Lord and of the holy Church.

I desire that this letter, which I wanted to write especially

* Pope John familiarly referred to his brother Zaverio (Xavier) as Severo. *Barba* in the local dialect means uncle.—Tr.

to you my dear Severo, be like a voice that reaches everybody, Alfredo, Giuseppino, Assunta, sister-in-law Caterina, your dear Maria, Virgilio and Angelo Ghisleni, as well as to all those who are related to our family, and that it be an expression of my ever living and ever youthful affection for them. Busy as I am, as you know, in a service so important that the eyes of the whole world are turned toward it, I cannot forget my dear relatives to whom my thoughts return day after day.

It is a joy for me to know that, since you cannot engage in personal correspondence with me as before, you can confide everything to Msgr. Capovilla who is very fond of you and to whom you can say everything just as you would to me.

Please remember that this is one of the very few letters that I have written to anyone of my family during the past three years of my pontificate. Please understand if I cannot do more, not even for blood-relatives. Even this sacrifice that I impose upon myself in my relations with you does you and me honor and gains more respect and sympathy that you can believe and imagine.

The great manifestations of reverence and of affection for the Pope on the occasion of his 80th birthday are coming to an end. I am glad of this because to the praises and good wishes of men, I prefer the mercy of the Lord who has elected me to so great a task and whom I wish will be a pillar of support to me up to the end of my life.

My personal tranquility which so impressed the world lies only in this trust. To be ever ready to obey, as I have always been, and not to desire or to pray to live longer, not even a day beyond the time in which the Angel of Death will come to call me and take me to heaven, as I hope.

This does not prevent me from thanking the Lord because he has willed to choose precisely in Brusico and Colombera the one who was to be called the direct successor of so many popes down the course of 20 centuries, and to assume the name of the Vicar of Christ on earth.

Through this call the name Roncalli was made known in the world and everywhere surrounded with sympathy and respect. And you do well to practice humility as I myself also try to do, and not let yourselves be impressed by the innuendoes and chatter of the world. The world is interested only in making money, enjoying life and imposing itself at whatever cost, unfortunately even ruthlessly if necessary.

The past 80 years tell me, as they also tell you dear Severo, and all the rest of our family, that what counts most is to hold ourselves in readiness to depart suddenly. The most important thing is to assure ourselves eternal life by trusting in the goodness of the Lord who sees all and provides for all.

I like to express these feelings to you, dearest Severo, so that you may transmit them to all our closest relatives of Colombera, Gerola, Bonate and of Medolago, and wherever they may live and whose place of residence I don't even know exactly. I leave the manner of doing this to your discretion. I think that Enrica could be of help to you, and Don Battista also.

Continue to love one another, all of you members of the new Roncalli families, and try to understand me if I cannot write to each individual family. Our Giuseppino is right when he tells his brother the Pope: "You are a prisoner of luxury who cannot do everything he would like to . . ."

I would like especially to remember the names of those among you who suffer most: dear Maria your blessed wife, and the good Rita who has assured herself a place in paradise with her sufferings, and for both of you who have assisted her with so much charity, and sister-in-law Caterina who always reminds me of her and our Giovanni who watches over us from heaven, together with our Roncalli relatives and closer relatives like those of the Milanese emigration.

I know very well that you will have to undergo some mortifications from those who talk without understanding. To have a Pope in the family, on whom the respectful gaze of the world is fixed, and to let them live so modestly without raising them in their social position. Meanwhile many know that the Pope, son of humble but honorable people, does not forget anybody, that he has and shows a good heart for all his closest relatives. And that, besides, his condition is that of almost all his most immediate predecessors, and that the honor of a Pope is not to enrich his relatives but only to assist them with charity according to their needs and the conditions of each one.

This is and will be one of the most beautiful and appreciated titles of honor of Pope John, and of his family, the Roncallis.

At my death the praise that so greatly honored the sanctity of Pius X will not be lacking: born poor and died poor.

It is natural that having completed my 80th year, all the others will follow me. Courage! Courage! We are in good

company. I always keep near my bed the photograph which
contains all our dead with their names written on the
marble: grandfather Angelo, *barba* Zaverio, our revered parents, brother Giovanni, sisters Teresa, Ancilla, Maria and
Enriva. Oh! what a beautiful chorus of souls who are waiting for us and praying for us. I always think of them. To remember them in my prayers gives me courage and infuses
me with joy in the trustful expectancy of joining them all together in the heavenly and eternal glory.

I bless you all together remembering all the brides who
came to gladden the Roncalli family or who have passed on
to increase the joy of new families of different names but of
the same feelings. Oh! the children, the children! What a
richness and what a blessing!

                                    Joannes XXIII, Pope

SPIRITUAL TESTAMENT

Venice, June 29, 1954

Being on the point of appearing before the One and Triune God who created me, redeemed me, who willed me to serve him as his priest and bishop, and who filled me with graces without end, I entrust my poor soul to his mercy. I humbly ask him forgiveness for my sins and my deficiencies. I offer him that little good which I succeeded with his help in doing to his glory, to the service of holy Church, to the edification of my brethren, although I am imperfect and insignificant. I implore him finally to receive me, like a good and pious father, with his saints into eternal blessedness.

I once more profess my whole Christian and Catholic faith, and my membership in and subordination to the Holy, Apostolic and Roman Church, and my perfect devotion and obedience to her august head, the Supreme Pontiff, whom I had the great honor to represent for many years in various regions of the East and West, who finally willed to appoint me Cardinal and Patriarch of Venice, and whom I have always followed with a sincere affection beyond and above every dignity conferred upon me. The sense of my littleness and of my nothingness has always kept me good company, keeping me humble and tranquil, and granting me the joy of practicing as best as I can continued obedience and charity toward souls and in the interests of the kingdom of Jesus, my only Lord. All glory to him. My merit is the mercy of the Lord. *Meritum meum misericordia Domini. Domine, tu omnia nosit: tu sciis amo te.* This alone is enough for me.

I ask forgiveness of all those whom I may have unknowingly offended, and of all those whom I may have failed to edify. I feel that I have nothing to forgive anybody for in all those who knew me and had contact with me— even if they should have offended or despised me or held me in dis-esteem, even justly so—I recognize only brothers and benefactors to whom I am grateful and for whom I pray and will always pray.

Born poor, but from honorable and humble people, I am particularly glad to die poor. In the service of the holy Church which has nourished me, I have given away, according to the various requirements and circumstances of my simple and modest life, whatever came into my hands— though to a very limited measure, for that matter—during the years of my priesthood and of my episcopacy. Appearances of affluence often veiled hidden thorns of a bitter poverty and prevented me from giving with the liberality that I would have wished. I thank God for this grace of poverty to which I took a vow in my youth, the poverty of spirit, as a priest of the Sacred Heart, and real poverty. It sustained me in never asking for anything, neither for posts, nor for money, nor for favors, never either for myself or for my relatives or friends.

To my beloved family *secundum sanguinem*—from whom, moreover, I have received no material riches—I can leave only a great and most special blessing, with the invitation always to preserve that fear of God which rendered them always so dear and beloved to me so that I never blushed with embarrassment over their simplicity and modesty. This is their true title of nobility. I have also helped them sometimes when their needs were more serious, as a poor man among the poor, but without removing them from their honest and contented poverty. I pray and I will always pray for their prosperity, glad as I am to observe a firm and faithful attachment to the religious tradition of the fathers also in the new generation. This will always be their good fortune. My most fervid wish is that none of my relatives or kinsmen may be missing in the joy of the final eternal reunion.

Departing, as I hope, for the paths of heaven, I greet, thank and bless the many who successively constituted my family in Bergamo, in Rome, in the East, in France, in Venice, and who were my fellow-citizens, benefactors, colleagues, students, collaborators, friends and acquaintances, priests and lay persons, religious and sisters for whom through the disposition of Providence I was, although unworthy, colleague, father or pastor.

The goodness which my poor person encountered from all whom I met on my journey rendered my life joyful and serene. In the face of death I think of all of them and of each single one of them, those who have gone before me, those who will survive me and who will follow me. May they pray for me! I will repay them from purgatory or from heaven where I hope to be received, I repeat once more, not because of my merits but because of the mercy of my Lord.

I remember them all and I will pray for them all. But as a sign of a wholly singular admiration, appreciation and tenderness I wish to make special mention here of my Venetians, the last whom the Lord set around me as the final consolation and joy of my priestly life. I embrace them all in spirit, all, the clergy and the laity, without distinction, just as I loved them without distinction as persons belonging to a same family, and as objects of a same paternal and priestly solicitude and lovingness: "Holy Father, keep in thy name those whom thou hast given to me, that they may be one even as we are" (Jn 17:11).

In the hour of saying goodbye, or better, of bidding farewell until we meet again, I still remind everybody of that which counts for most in life: Jesus Christ, his Church, his gospel, and in the gospel especially the Lord's Prayer in the spirit and with the heart of Jesus and of the gospel truth and goodness, meek and benign, industrious and patient, unconquered and triumphant goodness.

My sons, my children, until we meet again! In the name of the Father, and of the Son and of the Holy Spirit.

In the name of Jesus who is our love, in the name of Mary, our and his most gentle Mother, in the name of St. Joseph, my first and favorite protector. In the name of St. Peter, of St. John the Baptist, of St. Mark, of St. Laurentius Giustiniani and of St. Piux X. Amen.

Cardinal Angelo Giuseppe Roncalli, Patriarch

... the lines that I have written are to be considered as an attestation of my last will in the case of sudden death. Venice, September 17, 1957.

Ang. Gius. Card. Roncalli

My Testament

Under the dear and trustful protection of Mary, my heavenly Mother, to whose name the liturgy of this day is dedicated, and on the 82nd year of my life, I hereby depose and renew my testament, nullifying every other declaration regarding my last will which I have made and written earlier and on several occasions.

Calmly and gladly I await Sister Death. I shall accept her in accordance with all the circumstances that it will please the Lord to send her to me.

Above all I beseech the Father of Mercy for forgiveness for my *innumerabilibus peccatiis, offensionibus et negligentiis*, as I have so often said and repeated at the celebration of daily Mass.

For this first grace of Jesus, for all my sins and for the acceptance of my soul in blessed and eternal heaven, I recommend myself to the prayers for the repose of my soul of all those who have been close to me and who have known me during my whole life as priest, as bishop and as a humble and unworthy servant of the servants of God.

Then with an exultant heart I renew my whole and fervid profession of the Catholic, apostolic and Roman faith. Among the various forms and symbols with which the faith is usually expressed I prefer the Credo of the priestly and

pontifical Mass because of its special loftiness and lyricism
and its spread throughout the universal Church, in every
rite, in every century, and in every region, from the "*Credo
in unum Deum patrem omnipotentem*" to the "*Et vitam
venturi saeculi.*"

Sources

Letter to His Brother Zaverio, December 3, 1962, *L'Osservatore
Romano*, June 8, 1963.

Spiritual Testament, *L'Osservatore Romano*, June 8, 1963.

POPE PAUL ON HIS PREDECESSOR

Habemus Papam!

Announcement of the Election of John XXIII
October 28, 1958

To the Clergy and Faithful of the Archdiocese of Milan:

The announcement that Cardinal Angelo Giuseppe Roncalli, Patriarch of Venice, has been elected Supreme Pontiff under the name of John XXIII, which henceforth will be greatly revered and blessed by us, reverberates loudly and festively throughout Milan. It expresses the exultation of the whole Church that grips our minds as children of the great Mother and as brethren of the whole Catholic world. This connection, this consonance of the Ambrosian spirit with the universal family of Christ, this devotion and adhesion to the Apostolic See are characteristic notes of Milan's spirituality, vibrating in joyful unison in this momentous hour. If ever the aphorism of our St. Ambrose: *"Ubi Petrus, ibi Ecclesia,"* which one of his recent successors perfected further in the programmatic motto: *"Ubi Petrus, ibi Ecclesia Mediolanensis,"* could rightfully be proclaimed with fullness of spirit, now indeed is the hour to make it ours as a glorious sign of our history as a spontaneous cry of our minds, and as a filial commitment of our hearts. Once more we offer it as an eloquent expression of our sincerest homage to the newly elected Pontiff.

On this very happy occasion these considerations, expressing feelings shared by all Catholics and traditional Milanese piety, are supplemented by others of a particular and personal nature which move and gladden us in the depths of our being, impeding our faculty of expression: the Pope is a native of Lombardy, having been born in our nearby most fortunate diocese of Bergamo, sister in customs and faith to our own on so many grounds. It was in Milan that the Pope personally conducted historical researches which ultimately resulted in the publication, in five volumes, of the documents relating to the pastoral visit made by St. Charles to the diocese of Bergamo. In Milan the Pope's host and friend was our deeply mourned and revered Cardinal Schuster whose memorable, affectionate funeral oration he, already Patriarch of Venice, delivered in our cathedral. With the affableness that is native to him and with a great courtesy that does us a singular honor, the Pope always wished to maintain contacts of the most cordial and active character with our diocese, thereby making the binomial Venice-Milan tantamount to an expression of spiritual friendship based on a community of interests.

We desire, therefore, dear colleagues and faithful, to invite you all, collectively and individually, mentally to fuse our feelings into a common joy and to express them in a hymn of thanksgiving to the Lord for having bequeathed to his Church a Head who is wise, so good, and so beloved. And I invite you further quickly to transmute this thanksgiving into an avowal of devotion and loyalty to the Roman pontiff.

Our wish is that the wave of enthusiasm which invests us all, rather than distract us into a legitimate ebullient and festive mood, should compellingly invite us to a meditation, which now will seem new and true as never before, on the Church and the historic and highly significant episode in her history that we are enjoying today. We must feel, almost as a spiritual experience, the nature of the Church of Christ, this immense family of believers who possess this prodigious unity with respect to an attestation of Christ's love which gathers us all obediently around a visible Head, under an authority all the more to be celebrated as supreme the more it is recognized as vicarious. An authority, namely, which resolves into the exaltation of the only Head, Jesus Christ, now invisible, and which makes the person who fully exercises it the authority of the Servant of the servants of God.

Our wish is that the world of those who are distant from us, of the distracted, of the dissidents, of the indifferent, of the hostile, should look upon this phenomenon of human and superhuman beauty, of loftier hope, of easy access, and envy our joy in being Catholics so that they too might then share it with us.

Our wish is that we Catholics should deepen within ourselves the mystery of the Church and of the Pope, and that we live this mystery with greater awareness and with a love marked by a greater conviction, as a deep, fruitful and joyous reason for our modern spirituality. Especially we Ambrosians. It is for this that I joyfully bless you all, certain of making mine the gesture which the new Pope far away is already tracing in heaven for us all.

On the Election of John XXIII

ADDRESS DELIVERED IN THE DUOMO OF MILAN
NOVEMBER 1, 1958

Excellencies, Gentlemen, Colleagues and Faithful:

We are all gathered in our metropolitan Church in order solemnly to celebrate the election of the new Supreme Pontiff who ascends the Chair of Peter under the name of John XXIII. He continues in our time the unbroken apostolic succession as Vicar of Christ and thereby becomes the visible Head of the Catholic Church. He gathers the religious and civil legacy of the Roman popes—Bishop of Rome, Primate of Italy, Patriarch of the West, Universal Pastor, and prepares himself to exercise here on earth the supreme authority of the mysterious keys of the kingdom of the heavens. Teacher of the divine verities, unarmed sovereign, he rises over the whole world as a prophet of immortal hopes and, as a humble servant of the servants of God, as the first friend of humanity, he bows low in order to disclose to our life its real destinies.

These lofty considerations, almost of a crushing weight, render us incapable of giving you an adequate conception of this event, and of measuring its historic and transcendent reality. Yet they do not prevent us from pausing to dwell on

certain aspects which are more accessible and familiar to us
and which likewise invite us to this act of celebration. We
must, in fact, religiously and collectively manifest our joy
over this great event because of the position which the
papacy now occupies in the world and which leaves none
insensible to it among those who are aware of the values
operating for the peace and prosperity of nations. We
Italians, in particular, who have the singular good fortune
to provide hospitality to the geographical and historical See
of the papacy itself, we can also take pleasure in the fact,
never devoid of a profound significance, that this Pope too
is of the same nationality to which we also have the honor
to belong and which once more has been recognized as the
best suitable to exercise functions of a universal character
for the benefit of the whole of mankind. Further, we can
also take pride in the circumstances, so rich in human
associations, that Giuseppe Angelo Roncalli is a son of our
Lombard land, a loyal citizen of a tiny Bergaman town just
a few steps beyond the borders of our Milan diocese, to
which he came first as a priest and then as a scholarly
prelate in order to exhume, with infinite impatience, materials from the archives for his learned historical studies.

He who can already glory in some direct knowledge of
the person of the new Pope will add other reasons for satisfaction and for hope so as to give this ceremony a tone of
open-hearted cordiality, knowing how much serene goodness, jovial simplicity, human wisdom effortlessly pours
forth from the conversation of the new Pontiff in whom a
manifold and solemn experience and a consummate human-
istic and ecclesiastical culture have not inhibited the spon-

taneity of entertaining conversation and a facile vein of a subtle Manzonian wit.

Such observations and impressions fill our minds with contentment which we now wish to express by thanking the Lord who favors us with the grace of allowing us to witness the advent of the new Pontiff under the most felicitous signs: the perfect course of the millennial tradition which, before our eyes, proceeds tranquilly, confidently, regally in the succession from one great Pope to another who renews admiration, affection and hope around his own person, and those signs of wisdom, of goodness and of peace which already shine resplendently on the dawn of this pontificate.

This serene and majestic vision should awaken not a few auguries and prognostications in our hearts: what will be the course of development of the work of the new Pontiff? What would we like it to be? Perhaps each one of you feels not a few wishes and presages being born in his thoughts. But prudence wills and reverence imposes that they remain reserved in the heart, knowing well how vain and presumptuous it would be to give them expression. For what prevails over our short-sightedness is precisely the trust that the man chosen by the Holy Spirit will know how to accomplish things that are loftier and greater than those which our fantasy ingenuously might invent. If ever, therefore, our lips form a wish, it is that which hopes that the mission entrusted by Christ to the person who must represent him be one that is full, valid, long and felicitous: "Strengthen your brethren" (Lk 22:32); "Feed my lambs" (Jn 20:15); "Go therefore and make disciples of all nations" (Mt 28:19), and that it truly be conducted for the peace and for the redemption of mankind. It seems more advisable, rather, to dwell on another order of ideas. They are of a less spontaneous character, but all the more enjoined upon us in this moment which finds us all prepared to render homage to the new Supreme Pontiff. This concerns our relations with him, our duties toward the highest spiritual authority to which the divine plan of redemption has willed to bind all men under specifically established aspects. A celebrated definition comes to mind. Indeed, unforgotten, it pursues minds like a perennial question: ". . . subesse Romano Pontifici omni humanae creaturae declaramus . . . de necessitate salutis." We declare that for the salvation of every human being it is necessary that he be subject to the Roman Pontiff (Unam sanctam, Denz. 469). Truly the thought becomes grave, truly it presses upon every conscience and poses itself in the inner recesses of every mind which wishes to give a precise, central and decisive answer to the problem of its own destiny and to the religious problem. The question poses itself in direct derivation from divine thought, a thought of love that wills to save us in unity, that wills to reflect, on the human plane, something of supreme beauty, of supreme peace, of divine unity. Let us recall the sublime last prayer of Jesus: "That they may all be one, even as you, Father, are in me, and I in you . . . even as we are one" (Jn 17:21–22).

We cannot now proceed further along this marvelous and mysterious path. It suffices to mark it out. Let us note, nonetheless, how obedience to pontifical authority has a specific actuality in our time. Obedience, we said, is in line with a plan, an order, a unity. The modern world treads its way, indeed it is running toward forms of an increasingly more ordered and centralized character. We should welcome the fact that this magnificent phenomenon must be reflected also in the religious field. Once more we shall have occasion to see how the principles of progress and of civilization not only have a parallel exigency in the Catholic Church but find therein an anticipated and genetic exemplification. Recently, a most distinguished and authoritative scholar wrote these words: "Despite every residual incomprehension, every limited and selfish evaluation of interests, the world is being unified more and more and with an ever increasing swiftness . . . So keen and strong is the desire for unity that it also extends—and it could not have been otherwise—to every man's most personal sphere of which he is most guardedly jealous, namely that of faith. The signs of this ever more deeply felt exigency are multiplying" (N. Jaeger, It. ed. 28–X–1958).

Hence we Catholics especially must not be dismayed if the juridical organization of the Church in our time, especially after the publication of the Code of Canon Law in our century, evidences a marked centralization. The exercise of pontifical authority, of the inherent primacy of Peter, has become more frequent, more expeditious, perhaps even more demanding than it was in the past, when the means of communication and the need to give the Church a stronger and more organic internal cohesion were less than they are today. But this is progress. This is the Gospel that is being extended and asserted. This is charity that is being kindled in the great family of Catholicism and is being accelerated in a circulation of relations that endow the whole Church with vigor and splendor.

I say this because I think that after we have thanked God

for having given a new and saintly pontiff to his Church and a powerful worker for peace and civilization to the world, it is fitting that we Catholics offer the homage of our filial obedience to the Pope. We believe in his divine mission. We see in his authority an extension of the message of the Gospel. We know that a supernatural charism confers an infallible prudence on the Pope relating to matters of faith and to the guidance of our efforts directed toward our eternal destiny. We trust in his sovereign and disinterested love, which desires nothing else save our highest good. We know that we are needful of an illumined and strong guidance. We shall obey. Our obedience will be our commitment, our security, and our peace.

We shall obey also because ecclesiastical obedience, as we know, is respectful, indeed vindicative, of every other legitimate authority. It does not step beyond the sphere of its competence even when indirectly it produces repercussions in the temporal sphere. It does not create servants, but children. It does not desire inert or passive instruments; rather it awakens free and active consciences. So great is the confidence that this filial promise instils in our hearts that we feel no misgivings about combining it with the humble expression of our spontaneous desires: the Pope is a father, and nothing is kept from the father. Indeed, it is precisely in order to manifest our intention of loyalty that we look toward him with immense faith, and that we await vigorous and salutary utterances and directives, clear and compelling examples from him as we previously awaited them from his great predecessors.

May the Pope resume the teaching of principles. We

know quite well that he cannot give us the gifts of profane science, of political power, of earthly riches. But he can give us the gifts of wisdom. He can make light in the world with the simple and vigorous affirmation of the principles of which the Gospel is the codex, on which not only ecclesiastical life but modern life in general must be based, as on foundations.

May the Pope continue the work of peace which the pontiffs of recent times have so faithfully promoted, allowing the Church to savor the meaning of the living community of the charity and of the presence of Christ, ever more ardently desired, and teaching the world the paths of concord and justice which, if they are straight, all lead to Christ.

May the Pope read into the hearts of his children who, through a felicitous juncture, at this time seem to desire —whether they are docile or impatient—nothing better than that sanctity be the definitive subject matter of religious truth.

Sanctity: each in his own way, Catholic and non-Catholic, ponders it, and desires it conjoined with the great and mysterious mission of the Roman Pontiff.

May sanctity therefore be the augury, may it be the prayer that we shall recite today for "His Holiness" in today's stupendous feast of All Saints—a prayer which we shall also recite for ourselves, who await a better knowledge of the Pope's wishes from his mission and benediction in order the better to follow him along his path.

On Being Elected to the Cardinalate

Most Blessed Father!

The first feeling that is born in my mind, and certainly in the minds of the most worthy prelates whom you have summoned with me to form part of the Sacred College of Cardinals and whom you now see gathered around you, is one of veneration and of gratitude for your paternal goodness. It is this goodness that wills our presence here, that encourages us to assume an office of such great importance in the Church of God.

Already in these first weeks of your pontificate you, most blessed father, have desired to spread your goodness in broad and manifold ways, as though you were desirous of presenting yourself immediately to the Church and to the world under an aspect that seemingly purposed to define your august person and your apostolic work in a characteristic way, namely that benignity by which the divine Teacher wished to give an unmistakable sign of himself. Quickly the Church, quickly the world, their eyes fixed on the apparition of the new Vicar of Christ and their ears poised to listen to his utterances, have known how to gather those features of the evangelical image which in the gesture, in the character, in the very words of Your Holiness recall the figure and the program of the Good Shepherd. And quickly both the Church and the world were suffused by an arcane and agreeable wave of gladness and of trust.

We who have been given new, great and sovereign proof of so much goodness—extended also to the dioceses, the ecclesiastical offices, the nations and the faithful that, in various ways, we have the honor of representing or the responsibility of directing—now stand around you, deeply moved.

Your Holiness, almost in emulation and continuation of the goodness of your venerated predecessor of indelible and happy memory who desired to have each one of us occupy those posts which marked us out for your favor, without any delay have wished to show yourself solicitous and to provide for the fullness of the Sacred College and for the requirements of ecclesiastical governance. At the same time, you have wished to lavish on our persons the most generous and most expressive tokens of your magnanimous affability.

Thus we feel ourselves immediately committed to the comprehension of the great lesson of goodness which emanates from Your Holiness from these very first moments of your pontificate. Obedient to your example, we wish to make it the subject of our reflection and of our intentions.

Yours is a nimble goodness, most blessed father, which in a few days has already made Rome, the Church, the missions, the world thrill with welcome surprises. Meanwhile your spirited and open adherence to the easy-going speed which is peculiar to the style of the time notifies us that it is opportune to accelerate the advent of good as much as possible and to give the action of the Church, always with the requisite reflection and gravity, the expeditiousness called for today by the spiritual crisis of our society and by the urgency of its needs, and at all times by the law of charity.

Yours is an erudite goodness, most blessed father. It knows how to extract much from the patient, silent and searching perusal of documents, inherited from centuries past and slumbering in ecclesiastical archives, in order to bring about a renewal of useful studies of the Church, and from which it derives a living example of experience.

It is a sagacious goodness which, though indulgent to every dialogic encounter between man and man, surrenders nothing of the rights of truth and of justice. Rather, with a simplicity equal to prudence, it knows how to introduce amicable formulas of justice and truth which are neither weak nor equivocal by virtue of being polite and felicitous, but precisely good and knowledgeable.

Allow me to say further that yours is a vigorous goodness, most blessed father. It does not extend a trembling and hesitant hand to the wavering man, but one that is robust and paternal. How can we fail to recall your cordial and open call, on August 12, 1956, to your children, inclined to dangerous deviations? And it remained a vigorous goodness in the powerful and sorrowful speech delivered two days ago in the secret consistory, when the weeping voice of the Pope denounced evil and sincerely deplored the violation of the rights of religion, and no less those of freedom and of human dignity, for which every honest person ought to be grateful.

It is the goodness of Christ which your natural virtues of piety and of human sympathy sublimate in the art of drawing closer to the people, of understanding them, of commiserating with them, of admonishing them, and of opening their hearts to the revelation of the Christian vocation and of divine charity. A goodness which takes greater pleasure in giving to others and in suffering for them, rather than in having things and delighting in them for yourself.

But while we allow these rapid reflections on the form in which your divine mission assumes a human concreteness in your personage, to invest us from all sides, we feel a great trepidation mounting within us for having been called to become part of the senate which must concur and collaborate with Your Holiness for the good of the Church and of all mankind. It is the trepidation of perceiving that goodness, if such is the virtue with which your pontificate purposes to be exercised, obliges us to invest our persons, our labors with that evangelical style which, as we well know, is as attractive of admiration as it is difficult of imitation.

But your very goodness, Most Blessed Father, will be a comfort and an example to us. And as far as concerns myself, it will also be bountiful in indulgence and a constant spur. Our commitment shall be a great one so that the Church, as luminously as possible, may assume the majestic and gentle figure of the mother, of the "*pia mater*" in the words of St. Ambrose, indeed of the Holy Mother Church, before a world which, having lost faith in the Fatherhood of God, seems to give to civilization the impersonal and frightful aspect of a materialistic humanism. Thus do we come trustfully to the investiture of this most lofty office which Your Holiness benignly wishes to confer on us, with a firm and cordial resolve, with the help of God and the assistance of the Most Blessed Virgin, to repay you generously and devotedly.

Bless our persons, therefore, Holy Father. Bless all those who are our colleagues, children, collaborators in Christ. Bless also our good relatives and extend your apostolic blessing to the ecclesiastical offices, to the diocese, to the nations that it is our appointed destiny to represent here. And may you also preserve for all and grant to all the treasures of the goodness of Christ the Lord, whose august Vicar we recognize in you.

On the Installation of a
Bust of John XXIII

Certainly no one will inquire into the reasons why the Ambrosian Library has decided to celebrate the name and to perpetuate in its halls the features of Angelo Giuseppe Roncalli, now *fama super aethera notus* under the august appellation of John XXIII, our venerated and supreme Pontiff, happily reigning. In fact, the relations between this venerable institution and the Apostolic See are well known to all, being still close and active to this day. In order to solemnize today's commemoration of the three hundred and fiftieth anniversary of this most celebrated library, the Holy Father has deigned to nominate the Archbishop of Milan "*pro tempore*," in the humble person who is addressing you, as patron of the Ambrosian Library, almost as if to give thereby a tangible expression of his paternal interest and of his special benevolence, almost as if to make us aware of the loving solidity that marks our relations with the See from which he watches over us and attends to our needs. Thereby he is also granting a filial and most gracious wish that was expressed to him by the Most Reverend

Monsignor Prefect and by the Most Reverend Monsignor President of the conservatories of the Ambrosian Library, thus perfecting an important point of his earthly projects.

In confirmation of the vitality of these relations today, we have the honor to have present among us His Most Reverend Eminence Cardinal Eugene Tisserant, Dean of the Sacred College and Archivist of the Holy Roman Church, to whom we offer our most spirited thanks and special homage for the great honor he does us. We shall now have the good fortune to listen to his authoritative exposition of these same relations.

These reasons are very valid ones. But we know quite well that other reasons, of a wholly special character, must be conjoined to them. They tell us that the tribute which the Ambrosian Library pays to John XXIII, by installing a marble bust of the Pope in its sacred and silent confines, is not only a fitting homage, but one that duty enjoins upon us. Here, may it give to us and to posterity the pleasing impression of his spiritual presence, may it revive his memory, may it reflect the amiability of his smile and of his speech, may it offer the comfort of his example, and render this atmosphere—sacred to the silence of laborious study—richer in memories, more reminiscent of human and religious piety, and suffused more than ever with the mystery of noble sentiments.

John XXIII, in fact, himself was engaged in scholarly research here. By now it is generally known how, at that time, as a young priest and secretary to the great Bishop of Bergamo, Monsignor Radini Tedeschi, and as a professor at the Bergamo seminary, he frequented this library between 1906 and 1914. He was wholly taken up then with a great project, namely the publication of the documents of the apostolic visit made to Bergamo by St. Charles Borromeo in 1575. He had discovered these documents in thirty-nine weighty volumes bound in parchment in the archives of the archbishopric of Milan while waiting in the antechamber as his Bishop discussed preparations for the eighth Provincial Council with the venerable Cardinal Andrea Ferrari. This library was the scene of a memorable encounter, an encounter between two future popes. One agreed to make smooth the not so easy path of archival research for the other, and to trace the schema of the work, which was completed only last year with the publication of the fifth volume. Unlike the first volume, it was no longer presented by Monsignor Angelo Giuseppe Roncalli, but by John XXIII.

The author of the great work himself has written about that singular initial moment: "I still vividly recall my first encounter, timorous and uncertain, in that old consultation chamber in the corner on the right, way in the rear, where the Prefect received visitors with his customary polite and dignified amiability. I recall how his broad forehead registered his first impression before an idea that immediately appeared sound and interesting to him . . ." (Att. cit. I, xxxii–xxxiii). Two future Popes, Achille Ratti and Angelo Giuseppe Roncalli, came to know and understand each other here. Both studied here and made this library the spiritual workshop of their learned labors. It was here that the reigning Pontiff left the legacy, especially favored by him, of his patient research and the laboriously compiled publications. Setting a rare example of versatility and perseverance, he knew how to combine scholarly research with an external activity certainly not propitious to the silent labors of the library, but which dutifully was consecrated to the journeys, the ecclesiastical offices and services requested of him at first by the Roman Curia and later by the diplomatic representations of the Holy See, including even the pastoral cares of the patriarchate of Venice, i.e. on the very threshold of the Roman pontificate. When the first volume saw the light finally after more than twenty-five years had passed since the start of the enterprise, he himself wrote: "After such a long lapse of time, publication of the laborious research is now being resumed. I rejoice to see it return to that Ambrosian Library where the idea for it ripened and received its first and most authoritative impulse from the lips of Monsignor Achille Ratti" (*ibid.* xlii).

Thus we can well believe that Angelo Giuseppe Roncalli's contact with this library was neither superficial nor insignificant. Rather, it was very close, and the source of undying affections and lasting impressions. Here his mind, already predisposed thereto by his rich store of natural endowments and by the disciplines of excellent schools, was initiated into historical studies conducted at their primary documentary sources. Such studies educate those who devote themselves to them with particular speculative and moral virtues from which not only the psychology of the scholar, but that of the man and, we might add, even that of the priest, receives a characteristic imprint. They do not confer sheer virtuosity of memory and a varied erudition on the mind of the person who cultivates them with gravity of purpose and seriousness of commitment. Rather, such studies confer a capacity for mental order, an aptitude for the analysis of facts, of their causes, of their concatenation, and later an ultimate fitness for that synthesis which moderns customarily call history proper, namely a broad and organic view, never devoid of originality, of the human adventure and of the ideal principles that inform it. In this way, the experience of our forebears, expressed in time and flown with it, thus described, understood and spiritually relived, is transformed in some measure into our mental experience and illumines present judgment on human affairs, stimulating action on the basis of this or that choice taken with respect to a route that was traveled before. Thus is formed that "historical sense" which is such a large part of human experience and which is the reason why it is said that history is the teacher of life. That "historical sense" is one of the most fruitful motives inspiring to thought and action for us disciples who are participants in and ministers of God's mysterious plan in the world. It is the font of the knowledge of life and the stimulus to a trustful spiritual colloquy suffused with wonder.

That "historical sense," generally so deficient in the modern mentality, which is often ignorant of the past and wholly permeated by the present as it boldly strains toward the prognostications regarding the future without the slightest misgivings—that "historical sense" forms a fundamental virtue in the person who cultivates and possesses it. This is the cult of truth, scientific probity, the serious and honest use of the world restored to its responsibility of weaving sincere and intimate relations between human minds, enriched by its penetrating, expressive profundity.

Whoever notices how often the Supreme Pontiff in his addresses makes frequent reference to the necessity of restoring to the spoken and written word its genuine marvelous function as a scrupulous vehicle of the truth will not err, I think, if he traces this human and Christian wisdom, brought to such perfection, to the moral school of which he too was a pupil, and which has been in glorious residence here in the Ambrosian Library down through the centuries.

Hence the Ambrosian Library had to honor its son who became such a father to it. It had to call John XXIII to the concert of great minds who are the hosts and teachers of this incomparable cenacle of human and religious knowledge. It is most fitting that his paternal figure be here to recall his beloved and hidden history as an honest and zealous scholar, which ended in the glory of the Roman pontificate; to recall his example as a cultivator of our inexhaustible and still buried local memories; to comfort our vigilant love for St. Charles Borromeo, the model of post-Tridentine and modern pastoral action; to invite scholars from near and far to the perennial and renascent reawakening of this illustrious institution, priests especially, so that we can felicitously attain the aim—still valid today—of the founder of the Ambrosian Library, Cardinal Frederick Borromeo, namely "the formation of a specially instructed clergy which would serve to make the sacerdotal mission ever more useful and authoritative in society"—as the present venerable and worthy prefect of the Library superbly writes (181) in his biography of the founder.

It is most fitting, I say, that the paternal figure of John XXIII be here to receive our devoted filial homage. May our homage ascend to his holy and august person as a sign of the unshaken loyalty of this Ambrosian Library to the Chair of Peter. May it obtain from the amicable and Sovereign Pontiff his protective and stimulating blessing as a pledge of divine favor.

ON THE FEAST OF STS. PETER AND PAUL

MESSAGE TO THE CLERGY AND FAITHFUL
JUNE 16, 1961

To the Clergy and the Faithful of the Ambrosian Archdiocese:

We have just returned from Rome where we were called by the meeting of the Council of the Italian Bishops' Conference, and where we had the good fortune, ever new and ever moving, of two audiences with the Holy Father. Consequently, we feel duty-bound to communicate to the whole archdiocese the apostolic blessing which on this occasion also His Holiness has deigned to impart to our great diocesan family, which he also holds dear, to our institutions, to our associations, to our young people, to our workers, to the seminarians, to Catholic Action, to our publications which we presented to him, and also to our daily newspaper *L'Italia*; and, finally, in an all-embracing gesture and with an all-inclusive sentiment, to the whole Lombardian episcopate and to our entire region.

The goodness which the Holy Father desires to reserve for our Lombard land obligates us to be particularly grateful. The knowledge that he frequently takes delight in recalling, with loyalty and friendship, our places, our churches, our affairs and our persons, our problems and our labors, and that his benevolence and his prayer assist us with a vigilant and cordial interest, should make us appreciative of such great courtesy and of such great piety. And it should spur us to that devotion and that loyalty to the Supreme Pontiff which have always been a feature of Ambrosian spirituality and which in the present circumstances must give proof of a particular vitality, almost as a token of our filial response.

Hence the next recurrence of the feast of Sts. Peter and Paul, which will take place next Thursday on June 29, seems a propitious occasion for all of us to reaffirm our affectionate and firm devotion to the Vicar of Christ, joining the devotion to the Prince of the Apostles to the memory and the veneration of his living successor John XXIII, as is already the custom for such festivities in our archdiocese.

A special reason, the eightieth birthday of the Holy Father, should make the celebration this year a more fervent one. This topic gladdens us because of the felicitous longevity of the reigning Pontiff. It moves us deeply because of the vigor and the freshness of his apostolic activity, and it urges us to petition the Lord that he preserve, in vigor of mind and works, such a beloved and providential pontiff to his Church for many years to come.

Therefore, we invite the reverend pastors and rectors of the Church to arrange the celebration of the coming feast of Sts. Peter and Paul with great care, with a special remembrance and a special prayer for our common father in Jesus Christ, John XXIII.

We recommend to all the faithful that they match such

a homage of loyalty and piety with a filial, spiritual reciprocation. And we exhort all to make a more generous offering for Peter's Pence. As is well known, the whole Church, in homage to the Pope's eightieth birthday, is invited to contribute to the construction of two Roman edifices: the church dedicated to St. Gregory Barbarigo and the new college for lay students coming from mission countries. Milan, ever ready for every good work, ever loving of the Pope, must with its offerings give proof that its heart is in these good works and also with this Pope.

Happy to be celebrating this feast, so pious and significant in character, with our priests, diocesan and religious, and with our faithful, we greet you and bless you all.

On the Occasion of the Lombardian Pilgrimage for the Eightieth Birthday of John XXIII

Address Delivered at Rome
November 4, 1961

Most Blessed Father!

Before Your Holiness stand the participants in the Lombardian pilgrimage who have come to Rome on this beloved feast of St. Charles, patron of our region and in a particular way of Milan, in order to celebrate it with you, who are also a son of that blessed land. By selecting it as the momentous day of your coronation as Supreme Pontiff of the Catholic Church you have purposed to characterize your universal ministry by placing it under the protection and almost under the inspiration of that incomparable saintly teacher of pastoral zeal, illumined and honored by your studies no less than by your devotion. We have come here in order to celebrate this beloved feast with you. On the occasion of your eightieth birthday, marked by a ceaseless epiphany of apostolic activity and of paternal affableness, you merit that the faithful of the entire world make the deeply felt piety of their felicitations and vows converge on the Pope of ecumenical goodness. We celebrate it with you because these Ambrosians and these Lombards, an almost symbolic representation of all the people of that region, are the closest, the most affectionate, the most devout among all your children.

Your Holiness sees before you, standing next to me, several bishops of the Lombard region, the representatives of the metropolitan chapter of Milan, of our seminaries, of our urban and rural parishes, of our diocesan works, of our colleges, of our committees of Catholic Action and of their associations and religious, charitable and social activities.

A notable group of Milanese and Lombardian business men who form part of our group merits particular attention. They are led by the Honorable Origlia, courageous sponsor in Milan of the construction of a new parish church which will be dedicated to St. Francis of Assisi, patron saint of the merchants who prepared this pilgrimage to Assisi and Rome precisely in order to render homage to their saint and to beseech an apostolic blessing for their persons and their generous project.

Welcome, Holy Father, the visit of these four thousand pilgrims, accept their filial gifts, accept above all their homage of loyalty, devotion and affection. Your courteous reception will satisfy their desire to feel a reforging of the spiritual ties that bind them to the center, to the Head of Catholic unity, of Catholic truth, of Catholic charity.

In a world which, as a supreme achievement of the efforts and the progress of its civilization, seems to aspire to nothing else except to feel itself united in the organization of its most modern services, in the development of its scientific culture, in the security of its peaceful coexistence and instead—during these very days—trembles fearfully before the growing perils to its civil structure, to its safety and to its peace which it itself has created and unleashed, it is a supreme comfort, a supreme hope to those pilgrims to gather their persons and thoughts around you in this fortunate hour, around you, Vicar of Christ, and father of a universal brotherhood, teacher of a truth that does not err and does not vacillate, pastor intent upon making men good and friends with one another!

From you, Holy Father, come gifts much greater than those we have brought here, gifts for ourselves, for the Lombardian dioceses, for all the persons and the works that are dear to us. Now we await your word and your blessing.

During the Illness of John XXIII

Letter from Rome
May 31, 1963

I made the journey by air with the three brothers and with
the sister of the Holy Father, simple and venerable persons
who were summoned to pay their final farewell to their
brother, the Supreme Pontiff. We arrived in Rome after
10 P.M. and proceeded quickly to the Vatican. The little
group was ushered into the chamber of the august invalid,
and I with them. Besides Monsignor Capovilla, two nuns
and the Pope's priest-nephew were also present. His Holiness was now unconscious and breathed regularly with
closed eyes, his head lying inert against the pillows, like a
very tired person. I prayed at the side of our most venerable
Pope, then I dared to approach nearer and kiss his unmov-
ing hand.

Then several cardinals filed into the chamber, one after
the other: Taglia, Marella, Pizzardo, Antoniutti, Cicognani.
I myself led Cardinal Testa into the chamber. He was
overcome with emotion. As I left the chamber, wholly
suffused in a grave and reverent silence, my eyes fell upon
a very poignant scene: the three brothers and the sister of
the Pope were seated around their august brother's bed,

motionless and silent. Their heads were bowed but fixed on the invalid before them, as if to count his final breathings and to recall memories of their home village. Their faces wore an expression of the most serene human piety and religious devotion, sure of its faith before the overhanging mystery of death as if it were a solemn and benign event. Outside, near the threshold of the chamber which had gathered the last breath of Pope Pius XI and which will gather that of John XXIII, stood cardinals, prelates and doctors. Wholly absorbed by and included in the dramatic moment, they were exchanging edifying episodes and utterances of the dying Pope. He had been most lucid in mind and speech up to about 6 P.M., conscious of his state and utterly calm in the face of imminent death. He had addressed kind words to everybody. He had special comments for Rome, of which he called himself the Bishop, for the council, and for world peace.

People weep, pray and keep vigil with an immense spiritual tension, but their hearts are suffused with an ineffable emotion, almost of beauty and victory.

What a luminous epilogue to earthly life, what a presage of the life to come in paradise!

REFLECTION ON THE DYING POPE

ADDRESS DELIVERED ON THE
HOLY NIGHT OF THE GIAC
JUNE 1, 1963

Dearest young people!* And you adults who are united
with them in this hour of meditation and prayer! Welcome
to this enthusing annual gathering! In this hour of vigil,
full of festivities and mysterious silences, open your minds
to the reflection which alone—it seems to me—can now
fill them with poignant images, open them to fond and
inspiring recollections, to immense and luminous horizons,
to a reflection on the dying Pope. While we here are enjoying the throb of joy and life which this stupendous
gathering stirs in our hearts, his earthly existence is pain-
fully, piously drawing to an end. Our Father in Christ is
leaving us, the Head of our Catholic Church is succumbing
to the weight of years and to the assault of human infirmity.
The Pope, our Pope John XXIII, orphans us of his living,
most gracious presence!

It is a reflection that befits this marvelous feast whose
radiant dawn is adumbrated by this nocturnal vigil. For
today's feast, Pentecost, speaks to us of Peter, it shows him

* The GIAC is the youth branch of Italy's Catholic Action.

to us rising from his all-too-human frailty to assume his functions as Head of the nascent Church, full of his prophetic charism, the first and most authoritative charism, to inaugurate the Christian announcement: that intrepid and proclamatory testimony of the resurrected life of Jesus the Christ, and of his now irresistible mission of salvation in the world. Peter and his successor constitute a single story, a single authority, a single presence of Christ operative on earth. It is easy for us to descend from Peter to John by way of the unbroken chain of apostolic succession.

This reflection on the suffering and agonizing Supreme Pontiff is one that speaks to us of the Church which, by suffering with him, feels the profundity and the universality of her own life. It speaks to us of that Church which, by virtue of the Holy Spirit, was born on the day of Pentecost and emerged from the chrysalis of the first formation to which Jesus engendered her, and who after that quickly bestirred herself—preaching, celebrating, pouring forth, spreading, conquering. The Church, which we are, was being born one and indivisible, vigorous with life. Those first communities were stirred by the same apostolic ardor that would want to stir our consciences as aware and militant Christians, enkindling in them that fervor of Catholic action to which our hearts, still today, would want to give themselves.

If this reflection on the dying Pope fills us with a deep sadness and an inexpressible affection, it also imbues us with the faith, serenity and greatness of spirit with which he consciously and tranquilly confronts death and goes forth to meet that Christ of whom he has been the exemplary Vicar among us. This, dear young friends, obligates us, indeed it especially obligates us to gather up his testament, his legacy, namely his last solemn message, the message of peace.

Do you recall, are you familiar with the great encyclical *Pacem in terris* with which John XXIII, on the sacred day of love, Holy Thursday, spoke to the Church and to the world? Never, perhaps, in our time did a word of one man, a word of a teacher, a word of a leader, a word of a prophet, a word of a pontiff trumpet forth so loudly and so amicably over all the earth!

Well, then, tonight we must remember to make ours this word of the Pope. We must gather up this word as a beloved, jealously guarded and operative remembrance of this incomparable Pope. The word of peace. But let us be careful! The word "peace" is among those that are most used and abused. A superficial, hasty and insidious interpretation of this word could distort the meaning that the Vicar of Christ gives to it. The peace of the Pope is not merely a simple, courteous augury. Nor is it merely a precise and documented teaching. It is a view of life and of civilization, it is a commandment to us, and a commitment for us. It is a grave and solemn warning which we could translate as follows: peace is not enjoyed, but it is constructed, created. It is not the fruit of indolence, of inertia, of laziness, of hypocrisy, but of a wisdom full of light and strength which the Pope translates in his now celebrated quadrinomial when he asserts that peace is based on truth, on justice, on love, on freedom.

Do we wish to make ours the Pope's great message, and

to make it the inspiration and program for our lives as faithful children and as active Catholics?

The Pope warns us that peace, namely the ideal form of the life of humanity, is not self-engendered. It must be willed and created. Furthermore, peace is not created without an ideal order, which is the sure interpreter of a profound thought that penetrates into the nature of man and into human destinies, namely divine thought. And he will tell us that that we must all be seekers of this divine thought, and that the magisterium of the Church has the key to it. And he will admonish us, finally, that it does not suffice to have a taste for and the knowledge of peace. We must actively and generously make profession of it.

When the word of Christ: "Blessed are the peacemakers" was announced to us, to which that of the Pope echoes in our day, perhaps we doubted that it was a message for our times and for our minds. Our minds had been educated to a bellicose and heroic view of life. They had been taught to despise the weak and to rout compassion from our hearts as a feeling unworthy of the modern superman. They had been told that one could not really love one's country without despising and threatening other countries. Thus other teachers had instilled into us the mystique of revolution and of hatred as the only hope for ushering justice into the world, and they had based the advent of peace on the sacrifice of personal and spiritual values.

The Christian who appealed to the gentle and human peace of the Gospel was despised as faint-hearted and scoffed at as a utopian. It required the epoch of the atom bomb, that is to say, of the most terrifying prospect that history has ever presented, in order to induce people and thinkers and statesmen to return to the reflection on the ancient evangelical beatitude proclaiming peace as a felicitous, bold and lofty virtue.

This is the reflection to which I invite you, young people of 1963. It should be easy for us Christians and for those of us who are intent upon harkening to the last message of this teacher of goodness and of wisdom that John XXIII has been. We must shake off from ourselves every erroneous view! We must remember that every misfortune is born of fallacious thought, and every good of thought which is illumined by truth. Every incomplete or fallacious view of the world engenders neither civilization nor peace! It can not be engendered by the materialist view according to which economic well-being suffices (even though we must recognize the latter as necessary) to establish peace! Much less the even more materialistic view according to which a human and sincere peace can spring from class conflict and the subservient spirit. We must also remember, as something that is extremely important to us, the Pope's penetrating observation on the damages deriving from the dichotomy in the minds of those who call themselves Christians "between religious belief and the content of their temporal activity."

It is necessary that we reconfirm our faith in the teaching of the Church to whom the Lord has given a providential teacher in John XXIII, who once more, and magnificently, has taught us how the true supreme human questions coincide with and are resolved in the word of the Gospel of Christ.

Indeed, we shall reconfirm this trust on this very night. We shall make the commandment of peace which John XXIII bequeaths us to his memory and to his glory, our light and our strength for these days, still so stormy and bitter. May his spirit, lifted to the transparency of the integuments of flesh and time, accept this humble filial homage and validate our purposes with his still amiable and encouraging blessing.

Love of the Governance of the Church
and of the World

Address in the Duomo of Milan
Pentecost 1963

Here we are celebrating the joyful feast of Pentecost, the
feast of the Church, "mother of the saints, image of the
supernal city," but with sadness in our hearts: the Pope,
the Head of the Church is dying. Everyone feels the gravity
of the event. It is a grave event not only in itself, in its relation to history, to the life of the whole Church and of the
world, but one of enormous gravity to each and all of us,
to all those who have loved this Pope. And everybody loved
him because of his serenity, his simplicity, his joviality, his
courtesy, his closeness to the people, his predilection for
the humble, the imprisoned, the suffering, for his optimistic
character and for his religiosity—at once so pious and aus-
tere. In a word, they loved him for his goodness.

This was the reason why he was so popular: people
greatly appreciate finding their own feelings, their gestures, their words reproduced in the great. This is why he
is so greatly loved: at bottom this is worth more than
goodness. What confidence he inspired in everybody! No-
body felt him to be distant. There was always the certainty
of finding in him a word of esteem for everybody, a gesture

of encouragement, a thought of hope and of peace! He was imagined as he really was: incapable of offending, incapable of being offended, humble and superior always. Even those distant from the Church admired him for this, almost as if he were one who could do nothing else but interpret everything properly, and discover in every condition the opportunity for an act of trust and of courtesy. He was actually that which is said about him: a happy temperament who combined the native virtues of modest, honest, hard-working people with the fine, exquisite virtues of a solid culture and of a consummate religious spirituality. For the reason that he brought these natural and spiritual gifts to such lofty heights, to the supreme office of the governance of the Church and of the colloquy with the world, and for the reason that he gave this office an informal cordiality and warmth, he has earned a universal affection as a true and rare friend of mankind. This is why every heart is gripped with trepidation and there is great weeping. One suffers when one loves.

I shall not make mention of the rest, which would be the more, namely of his work, of which the convocation of the ecumenical council and with the two great encyclicals *Mater et Magistra* and *Pacem in terris* have left a deep mark on the history of the Church and of civilization. Rather than mark it would be better to say a furrow, and one of an incalculable fertility. In a word, a good and grand Pope. We Ambrosians could say further: a Pope who is one of ours. How he loved Milan and St. Charles! His devotion, indeed his veneration for our saint, is proverbial to the point where he awakened in us, too, the intention of deepening the studies concerning him, to reanimate the

piety, now slightly tepid, which instead we owe to him as
a perennial filial duty. As the Pope expressed it in his last
message to us, he was "at home in Milan." He wanted the
canonization process of the servant of God, Cardinal Ferrari, to be promoted with greater alacrity. There was no
end to his recital of the episodes that had interwoven the
life of our incomparable archbishop with his own. He spoke
about our archives and our Ambrosian library as things that
were beloved and dear to him because he had unearthed
their secrets and treasures and because he had published
their documents in five weighty volumes, about which he
did not conceal his pride. And the Madonna del Bosco?
She was the Madonna of his childhood: he made a visit to
her artistic and rustic sanctuary each time he returned to
his native village. As Patriarch he placed a crown upon her
effigy, and as Pope he adorned it with a precious necklace.
It was not for nothing that the faithful of the sanctuary,
ourselves included, wanted to erect the most beautiful
statue on the picturesque flight of steps that lead up to the
sanctuary. Among us it will remain a monument to his
paternal and pontifical personage. He is one of ours and
for this, too, we have reason to be sad and deeply moved.

One suffers—I said—when one loves. But you, dear
faithful and colleagues, who have certainly, and with trepidation, followed the agonizing hours of the Pope's illness
and of its last awesome phase through the mass-media of
our modern world must have also experienced another
indefinite and complex feeling comingled with the feeling
of suffering, that feeling, namely, which the believer must
have in the face of a Christian death: a feeling of mystery,
to be sure, but also of trust, of complete surrender and

almost of joy. The joy of the hope and of the anticipation of the encounter with Christ, with his mercy and his glory. I do not wish now to give a chronology of these anxious and hallowed hours that marked the great and tranquil twilight of Pope John XXIII. You know it. It suffices to recall one word which he said to one of the doctors, who reported it to me, for us to perceive the atmosphere of spirituality that envelopes the demise of this great man of God. Referring to the inexorable malady that is bringing his earthly life to a close amid cruel sufferings, he replied to the doctor's commiserative question: "Are you suffering for pain, Holiness?" with the words: "Yes, but also for love."

And his love is God, the Church. It is the world. Indeed, we cannot avoid the pain, certainly beneficial to us, of witnessing the supreme separation of death, but we must do so without fear, without desperation, and with a balm of sweetness in the depth of our hearts which we Christians should know intimately and which we must gather with gratitude as a final paternal gift, as a lesson to be remembered, from the bedside of this dying Pope.

But why do I speak so much about him to you, and not of today's feast? Must you commiserate with the heart which at this time prevails over the mind? No, I think that the goodness, of which Pope John XXIII leaves us such an eloquent and moving manifestation, may be of service to us in understanding one of the aspects of Pentecost, an aspect which that goodness endows with actuality before our very eyes. It is an apology and almost a final attestation of the event that had occurred at that time.

In fact, what had occurred at that time was the entry

of love—the primal and living love, the love by which God himself is defined, the love proceeding and emanating from eternal God the Father thinking himself and from the Son, his Word, his thought and substantial image, in an act of reciprocal infinite graciousness, the love, that is, that we call the Holy Spirit. Love entered into the life of several men and electrified it. And through them it entered as a supernatural active and novel presence in the history of the world. It created the new humanity, creating in it at the same time a mystical participation in divine life, the state of grace, the state, that is to say, of God's new love for us, of his love and ours together. And the Spirit created the authority to communicate and transmit such participation, the authority to give it a social structure, to sanctify it, in other words, to govern it. It created the Church and in her the propelling organ which was to invest this participation with life. Truly, this was a phenomenon effected conjointly by the three divine Persons, but since it was a phenomenon of love it has been attributed, and rightly so, to the Holy Spirit. St. Thomas says: "*Amor quo diligimus Deum est repraesentativus Spiritus Sancti,*" the love by which we are rendered fit for the dilection of God is representative of the Holy Spirit (IV *contra Gentes* 21). But what is important to note is that that outpouring of divine life was a work of love, and gave a soul to the Church. "What the soul is for the body of man," says St. Augustine, "the Holy Spirit is for the body of Christ, which is the Church. The Holy Spirit effects in the whole Church that which the soul does in all the members of the body" (*Sermo* 267:4). Thus love became the animator of Christian civilization.

It is not difficult to see that an intrinsic kinship can exist between love, charity and goodness, so that the great actions that bear witness to and promote the life of the Church are effects of divine love, that is to say, of charity, which in human utterance is manifested as goodness. Everything in the Church is a work of charity and of goodness. Her magisterium, her word is charity, which kindles faith and initiates our supernatural regeneration. Charity is grace that is transmitted to us in the sacraments; charity is the hierarchy that dispenses these divine gifts. Charity becomes the history of the Church, promoted by that unique animation, by the Holy Spirit that pervades her entirely. This is Pentecost, a stupendous event that manifested itself more decisively and actively in the life of humanity than any other event, and which perdures to this day.

Thus we can console ourselves by recognizing in the humble and great figure of John XXIII the manifestation, more accessible and more evident to us than any other, of that goodness which is the intrinsic style and the effect of the divine charity animating the Church. That the highest authority of the Church should give us an example of an even more human goodness is by itself an ordinary fact, so essential is it that the authority of the Church be charity, love, ministry, gift, fatherliness, providence, sacrifice, goodness. But that such a coincidence of authority with goodness makes both shine resplendently at the apex of the Catholic hierarchy is a faithful and consoling attestation of the Spirit that ever and now animates the Church of God, and corroborates and sanctifies him who functions in the Church as the Vicar of Christ.

Blessed, therefore, be this Pope who has given the image

of pastoral goodness to us and the world and who has made himself the evangelical example of the Good Shepherd to those who are responsible for the governance of the Church. Blessed be this Pope who has shown us that goodness is not weakness and flaccidness, nor an equivocal irenism, or a renunciation of the great rights of truth and of the great duties of authority. Rather, he has shown us that goodness is the principal virtue of him who represents Christ in the world. Blessed be this Pope who has once more made us see that the authority of the Church is not an ambition for domination, it is not remoteness from the community of the faithful, it is not a stylized and external paternalism, it is not that which the enemies of the Church or lay persons hostile or alien to her would want to qualify it as: namely a retrograde dogmatism impeding the progress of the world. Rather, it is a prudent and sagacious solicitude, a function willed by Christ, irreplaceable and worthy of every reverence and loyalty. But it is a humble, disinterested, laborious and cordial ministry which in its clearest and most authentic manifestation we can all majestically call goodness. Blessed be this Pope who has let us enjoy an hour of spiritual paternity and familiarity, who has taught us and the world that humanity needs nothing else so much as it needs love. Blessed be this Pentecost, at once sad and sweet, which in the human agony of John XXIII still shows us where the primal, the true source of love lies: in the Church of Peter.

Announcement of the Death of John XXIII

Message to the Clergy and Faithful
June 3, 1963

The very sad and very pious announcement of the death of His Holiness John XXIII, which took place today and which was awaited and feared in the days preceding his sorrowful and saintly demise, must find an echo of profound spiritual emotion in our minds as children of the Catholic Church, which weeps over the disappearance of her most beloved Head, as brethren of all the believers of the earth, who feel they have been orphaned of an incomparable father and teacher, as citizens of a world who recognized in the deceased Pope a friend of mankind, and as Ambrosians who have always enjoyed his loyal and cordial predilection for us.

It is the Pope of the Council who has died, the Pope of the social encyclical *Mater et Magistra*, the Pope of the encyclical *Pacem in terris*, which traces the lines of a modern and human coexistence. A great Pope, a Pope of simple and candid heart, of benign and good character, a Pope who marks a point of friendly and felicitous light in the history of the Church and of the world.

So much has been said about him, and so much will certainly still be said about him. Yet we must all formulate an intention in this most bitter and most lucid hour: to reflect once more on the figure and the work of the pontiff who has called for a deeper self-consciousness in the Church, and of the mission which Christ is continuing in the Church herself. Thus he has awakened immense spiritual energies within the bosom of the Church which vividly reveal her to us and to contemporary and future historians as youthful and strong, with the Christ whom she bears within herself, youthful and strong because of the powerful and inexhaustible dynamism of the human and transcendent values of which she is both the depository and the dispenser.

We would have to reflect again on this pontificate as a great phenomeon of inner Catholic regeneration and of external capacity for dialogue and common salvation.

And we invite you to another duty: to pray, to pray for his eternal peace, to pray for the Church and for all mankind. We do not doubt that you will be solicitous in the accomplishment of these filial duties in order to render a fitting tribute of honor and of remembrance to the venerated Pontiff, and in order to give our sorrow the only consolations that can mitigate it, that of the communion of saints, of the certainty, in other words, of a higher destiny of our mortal life in Christ, and that of Christian wisdom, which makes of example and commitment and love a treasure of lofty and sacred remembrances.

We present, therefore, the various dispositions acquiescent to this mournful event, certain of your response to our feelings and to our desires; united in sorrow, hope and prayer, we heartfully bless you.

From the Letters and Speeches of Pope Paul

At the beginning of our pontifical ministry the remembrance of our predecessors who have bequeathed as a sacred and glorious legacy lovingly and pleasingly comes to mind: Pius XI, with his indomitable strength of soul, Pius XII, who has illumined the Church with a teaching full of wisdom, and finally John XXIII, who has given the example of his singular goodness to the whole world.

But in a wholly particular way we love to recall, in moving and grateful devotion, the figure of our greatly mourned John XXIII who, in the brief but highly intensive period of his ministry, knew how to win over the hearts of men, even of those distant from the Church, by virtue of his ceaseless solicitude, his sincere and concrete goodness toward the humble, by virtue of the distinctly pastoral character of his activity, all qualities to which was added the wholly particular charm of the human gifts of his great heart. The radiant influence that he exercised on souls was a procession of illuminations following upon illuminations, like an ardent flame, up to the supreme sacrifice of himself. He endured this sacrifice with that fortitude that has stirred the world, gathering all men around his bed of suffering, as it were, and making them "cor unum et anima una" in a single throb of great respect, veneration, and prayer.

(From his first radio message, "Urbi et Orbi," June 22, 1963)

* * *

Venerable Brethren:

Now that the opening day of the second phase of the Second Vatican Ecumenical Council approaches, we cannot but feel deeply stirred by the greatness of that sacred legacy that has been transmitted to us by our predecessor John XXIII of venerable memory. A legacy that we have received, as you well know, trepidly and deferentially, prepared to refuse no travail whatsoever, no discomfort whatsoever, in order that this most precious treasure of works and instructions with which that great pontiff has enriched the Church may remain absolutely intact.

Undoubtedly the celebration of the Second Vatican Ecumenical Council that has already been initiated belongs to that treasure. Such an enterprise is so majestic in dimension that it can be considered among the greatest benefits with which John XXIII has enriched the Catholic Church and human society.

* * *

It was certainly through an arcane plan of divine Providence that the Pope, who had sown the terrain with the seed of such a great enterprise, was not able to gather the ripened fruits, imposing on us, instead, the task of continuing that work which had begun with provident wisdom, great fortitude and solid hope.

Upon reconsidering the dimensions of the task imposed on us, we feel a certain reluctance at undertaking the formidable work were it not evident that the will of God appears manifest therein. Hence we have viewed it to be our duty to assume the task and to obey the divine will, absolutely placing our trust in the Lord and hoping firmly that he will sustain our weak forces after having entrusted us with the accomplishment of so great a task.

Moreover, venerable brethren, your work will not fail to come to the aid of our labors which, we know well, will be of valid assistance to us. Upon undertaking this work, neither shall we be lacking in the vows and prayers of the faithful, bound to us by close ties of love in this great hour of the Church. This is a great comfort to us and it also seems like a felicitous augury for the prosperous success of the ecumenical council.

Because of the vast scale of work that the next phase of the council will involve, and because it deals with an event that touches on the life of the Church in the depths of her being, we ardently exhort you, venerable brethren, that you spiritually prepare the flock entrusted to each one of you. Following in the footsteps of our predecessor John XXIII, who never wearied of admonishing the Christian people to entreat God for abundant fruits from the council, especially through prayer and penance, we strongly recommend these important works of piety to you. The four

Tempora of autumn, now imminent, offer a propitious occasion for undertaking them.

(From the apostolic exhortation *"Cum proximus,"*
September 14, 1963)

* * *

Having a great understanding of the signs and the needs of modern times, our predecessor John XXIII, whose pious remembrance is ever green, with intrepid and trusting spirit undertook the majestic work of the Second Vatican Ecumenical Council. There is solid ground to believe that in this he was inspired by the particular impulse of divine Providence, which "sweetly disposes everything" (Wis 8:1) and with supreme wisdom provides for the welfare of the Church according to need.

The great interest and the high hopes that this ecumenical council, of such vast dimensions, has aroused among people and what immortal glory has resounded to the name of Pope John XXIII, sponsor of this great undertaking, is well known. He, who had dedicated all his energies to such a work and had himself celebrated the first phase of the council, through the inscrutable plan of God, was surprised by death, to the immense sorrow of the faithful and also of non-Catholics. There is no doubt, however, that, having humbly conformed to the divine will, he obtained, upon departing the earthly exile, an abundance of celestial graces on the Church, having offered his life to God for the felicitous outcome of the council.

We who have become his successor, through the arcane disposition of divine Providence, and trusting in the work and in the help of the council Fathers, have accepted his legacy in the name of God. Desiring, therefore, to continue with alacrity what was fervently undertaken, with this letter, venerable brethren, we convoke you to continue the Second Vatican Ecumenical Council, whose new period will begin, as you well know, next September 29.
(From the Epistle to the Bishops of the Catholic world,
            "Horum temporum," September 14, 1963)

* * *

Venerable Brother:
  Greetings and apostolic blessing.
  In accordance with the requirements of our apostolic ministry, since the beginnings of our supreme pontificate we have turned our attention to the Second Vatican Ecumenical Council whose second phase, as is known, we have disposed be begun this coming September 29, feast of St. Michael the Archangel, patron of the Church militant.
  This intention is due above all to the remembrance of our predecessor John XXIII, of venerated memory. We consider him as sent by God so that the Church could celebrate an event of such importance as an ecumenical council, and so that he might initiate it in the circumstances and according to the criteria known to all, and so that he would be the first to celebrate its providential, mysterious greatness. Oh! how daring and happy he was in

such a project and how great was his glimpse of its salutary fruitfulness, how great was his desire that the spiritual function of the Church in history and the world be recognized and celebrated so that all could realize the advantage for the future destinies of the Church and of mankind. How great must have been his sacrifice at not being able to see its development and conclusion in this life, after its first vicissitudes.

We are immensely grateful to God who has given us such a lovable Supreme Pastor of the Church, as a supreme gift. In the candor of his simplicity, in the splendor of his virtues, in his tenacious effort to foment peace, he not only filled the whole world with love and admiration for his person but, in addition, by his convocation of the ecumenical council, he has opened new paths to the redemptive activity of the Catholic Church. May the most merciful God that grant such a great work, begun by Pope John, arrive at a felicitous outcome and not delay the dawning of that resplendent day for the Church and the world of which he, thinking of the ecumenical council, glimpsed the dawn.

Deprived of so great a Supreme Pastor of the Church through the inscrutable design of Providence, and our soul filled with great trepidation and almost anguish, it came to pass that the weight of the governance of the Roman and universal Church was imposed on our shoulders, so unequal to so great a burden. A weight which burdens us all the more because it also involves the responsibility for continuing the ecumenical council already begun. We openly confess that it is not without fear that we feel the

weight of this duty. We are terrified by the weakness of
our forces, the great commitment of its celebration, and
finally by the grave problems of our era.

(From the letter to the Cardinal Deacon,
"Quod Apostolici," September 12, 1964)

* * *

We cannot think about this event without remembering
our predecessor of happy and immortal memory, John
XXIII, most beloved by us. His name re-echoes in us and
surely in those of you who had the good fortune to see him
here in our own place, his amiable and hieratic figure, when
on October 11 of last year he opened the first session of the
Second Vatican Ecumenical Council, and delivered that
speech which appeared like a prophetic voice to the Church
and to the world—a speech which still echoes in our
memory and in our consciousness—in order to mark out to
the council the path it was to follow, and in order to free
our minds from every doubt, from every weariness that
might overtake us in the arduous journey that had been
embarked upon. Oh, beloved and venerated Pope John,
may thanks and praise be rendered to you who, through
divine inspiration, we do believe, willed and convoked the
council, thereby opening new paths to the Church and
letting new waves of hidden and freshest waters of the
doctrine and of the grace of Christ the Lord pour forth
on the earth. You, urged on not by any earthly stimulus,
but almost by your divination of celestial counsels and by

your penetrating awareness of the obscure and tormented needs of the modern age, picked up the broken thread of the First Vatican Council. Thereby you spontaneously disabused the unjustified diffidence of some which derived from this council, as though it had decreed that henceforth the supreme powers recognized as conferred by Christ upon the Roman Pontiff sufficed to govern the Church without the help of ecumenical councils. You summoned the brothers, the successors of the apostles, not only to continue the interrupted study and the suspended legislation, but also to feel a unitary body united around the Pope in order to be comforted and directed by him *"ut sacrum christianae doctrinae depositum efficaciore ratione custodiatur atque proponatur"* (AAS 1962, 790). Indicating thereby the highest purpose of the council, you set before it another more urgent purpose and one now more salutary, the pastoral purpose by affirming: *"Neque opus nostrum, quasi ad finem primarium, eo spectat, ut de quibusdam capitibus praecipuis doctrinae ecclesiasticae disceptetur . . . ,"* but rather: *"ea ratione pervestigetur et exponatur, quam tempora postulant nostra"* (ibid. 791–792).

You revived in the consciousness of the ecclesiastical teaching office the conviction that Christian doctrine must not only be a truth to be investigated with the illumined reason of faith, but a word generative of life and action; and that the authority of the Church should not limit itself, merely to the condemnation of errors that offend her, but must be extended to proclaiming positive and vital teachings which she possesses in fruitful abundance. Neither merely theoretical, nor merely negative, the ecclesiastical teaching office in this council must manifest more strongly the vivifying virtue of the message of Christ who said: "The words that I have spoken to you are spirit and life" (Jn 6:63). Therefore, we shall not forget the instructions that you, the first Father of this council, wisely marked out for it and which it is useful to repeat here:

". . . *nostrum non est pretiosum hunc thesaurum—doctrinae scilicet catholicae—solum custodire, quasi uni antiquitati studeamus; sed alacres, sine timore, operi, quod nostra exigit aetas, nunc insistamus, iter pergentes, quod Ecclesia a viginti fere saeculis fecit.*" Therefore: "*eae inducendae erunt rationes res exponendi, quae cum magisterio, cuius indoles praesertim pastoralis est, magis congruant*" (AAS 1962, 791–792).

Nor shall we neglect the great question of the unification in a single fold of all those who believe in Christ and who yearn to be members of his Church which you, John, have pointed to as the house of the father opened to all in such a way that the course of this session of the council, which you promoted and inaugurated, may proceed with faithful adherence along the paths that you have marked out. And with the help of God may it arrive at the goal which you so ardently desired and hoped for.

(From the allocution to the council Fathers
at the beginning of the second session of the
Second Vatican Council, September 29, 1963)